I0820907

# Sabor y Fuego

## THE ART OF AUTHENTIC MEXICAN SALSA

# Sabor y Fuego

## THE ART OF AUTHENTIC MEXICAN SALSA

SONIA MENDEZ GARCIA

weldonowen

# Contents

## CHILES SECO

***Dried Chiles***



## SAUCES & ADOBOS



## TAQUERIA-LA TAQUIZA

***Taco Party***

# Introduction

My name is Sonia Mendez Garcia. I was born and raised in Southern California, with a large extended family living in Monterrey, Mexico. Little did I know that those five a.m. trips to Blanca's Mexican Food with my dad, Ramiro, would lead me here. It was always my dream to write a salsa cookbook. My Mexican-born parents, Ramiro and Blanca, owned Blanca's Mexican Food for a few years in the early eighties. I was only fifteen at the time, and my job on the weekends was to prepare fresh salsa for the weekend tacos. What seemed like a chore back then is something that I grew to love and became very passionate about. Mom cooked mostly homestyle traditional Mexican dishes six days of the week. Her salsa recipes were simple and mostly on the spicy side. This is where I came to appreciate spicy salsa, and still do to this day. From that experience, I officially took over the salsa preparation at the restaurant as well as at home.

I was married at age twenty-one and officially left my parents' home only to find myself across the country in a small town in New York state. The salsa preparation almost came to a complete stop, as there were minimal to no real fresh Mexican ingredients to be found. Mom would literally ship me care packages filled with serrano peppers, avocados, and limes. I can laugh about it now, but at the time I was desperate to see, smell, and enjoy those flavors and aromas that reminded me of home.

Mom had no written recipes, so basically, I was going by memory when it came to learning the family dishes. Thank goodness for my sisters; sister-in-law, Janet; cousins; and *tias* — all of whom shared information and memories of different dishes with me. I will always remember the first time I attempted to prepare tamales and *chiles rellenos* on my own! Oh, what a production it was! I can honestly say that it took me twenty years to finally feel confident when it came to preparing flour tortillas. Practice is the key!

Nowadays, I can walk into my kitchen and find all the ingredients to pull off a small batch of tamales within a few hours. Every fall, when I prepare that first steamer-pot filled with Mom's pork tamales, it is so exciting for me. That first bite always makes me cry. I often wonder if that happened to her, because she missed her home and mother, my *abuelita*.

My passion for cooking everything Mexican led to teaching cooking classes at the local kitchen supply store. It was a great experience and really brought me out of my shell. I was extremely shy, and talking in front of people terrified me. My first attempts at writing recipes were not good. Because I am detail-oriented, the recipes read like a script — way too long! And they were all handwritten, because at the time, I didn't know how to use a PC.

The students were eager to learn about Mexican dishes, and I made some wonderful friends. The price of one class included an appetizer, a first course, a main course, and dessert. It was a lot to accomplish in one evening, but we always managed to get everything done. For one year during that time, I challenged myself and served a Mexican lunch every Friday at the kitchen supply store. Fiesta Fridays! Unfortunately, small-town New York was not yet ready for authentic Mexican food. It involved a lot of work but was so much fun. I am unbelievably thankful for those years of teaching cooking classes and hosting Fiesta Fridays. They prepared me for the next step of my food journey, which was an open road!

After many years of working in retail, I found myself sidelined at home because of health issues. What was I going to do? Luckily for me, I stumbled upon an online community, the Hispanic Kitchen. It was there that I officially began sharing family recipes, including salsa recipes, with a wide audience. This experience led to my first job as a recipe developer for a number of Hispanic websites; I even became resident chef for one of the sites. The owner of the Hispanic Kitchen stated, "Girl, you came in like a hurricane sharing recipes!"

Jorge Bravo, the then-owner, gave me great tips on photographing food in natural light. He also gave me my first paid work as a food blogger, which is how I initially connected with a large following on social media. Friends and family encouraged me to start my own food blog, and, in February 2014, La Piña en La Cocina was born. *Piña* means "pineapple" in Spanish, and it is the childhood nickname my father gave me. The name stuck, and my family to this day calls me *Piña* or *Piñita* (little pineapple).

*Sabor y Fuego: The Art of Authentic Mexican Salsa* is the culmination of my more than forty-five years of cooking and testing recipes with ingredients that I love and feel very passionate about. You will find not only salsa recipes that I prepare regularly but also adobos, sauces, tortillas, and a few other surprises! The ingredients are readily available in most Mexican markets, supermarkets that carry international foods, and online. The recipes are simple, straightforward, and easy to follow. They will take you on a journey where you will learn and experience Mexican chile peppers, both fresh and dried. The cooking techniques and methods are traditional and authentic to me. Every family, every region of Mexico, has its own cherished recipes and cooking methods. Which is why I never call myself an expert at preparing salsa, because there is always something new to learn!

Each section of the book focuses on something a little different when it comes to preparing salsas, sauces, and adobos. **Salsa Fresca (Fresh Salsa)** features salsa recipes prepared with mostly uncooked ingredients or ingredients that require very little cooking time. There are a few *molcajete* recipes, quick blender recipes, and hand-chopped recipes. **Salsa Guisada (Cooked Salsa)** shares a series of salsa recipes where the ingredients are all cooked. The cooking methods range from gentle boiling to roasting on the stovetop. The recipes may combine boiled ingredients with roasted or toasted ingredients. **Chiles Seco (Dried Chiles)** highlights the variations of dried chile pods that I routinely use in my cooking. I really want to showcase the versatility of each pepper variety! Each salsa is unique in how it looks and how it tastes.

Recipes for **Sauces and Adobos** are a bit more involved. The sauces and adobos are mainstays in preparing and achieving dishes with traditional flavors. The chile peppers range from fresh to dried, and fresh produce is required. **Taqueria–La Taquiza (Taco Party)** comprises recipes that are not salsa. Pickled jalapeño peppers with carrots, red onion with habanero, corn and flour tortillas, fresh guacamole with homemade chips, and *chiles toreados* with *cebollitas*. These are all must-haves for a complete *La Taquiza* taco night!

Oh, and I haven't forgotten to include some favorite taco recipes!

Who doesn't enjoy tacos *de carnitas* with *pico de gallo* and *salsa cruda*? Perfectly blackened fish fillets with a smoky mango salsa? Tender *nopalitos* (cactus paddles) in a spicy salsa? The oh-so popular *birria*, the *barbacoa de cachete*, and cheesy shrimp tacos so delicious they even impressed the governor of Sinaloa! I could go on . . . and I do! Keep reading . . .

# Inside the Mexican Pantry

**What is essential to a Mexican kitchen? (I discuss this on my blog all the time.) Let's start with the pantry must-haves: fresh and dried chiles, spices, nuts, seeds, dried fruits, Mexican chocolate, vegetables, and fruit.**

## CHILE PEPPERS

Chile peppers have been cultivated in Mexico for thousands of years. Today, at least sixty varieties of chile peppers are grown in Mexico, although it's thought that there could be many more. The recipes in this book use the most common Mexican chiles and those readily available in the United States.

So, how hot is hot when it comes to chiles? The Scoville scale measures the concentration of capsaicin, which is what causes the heat sensation you feel when eating peppers. The rate of heat units is: Mild (100–500); Medium (1,000–1,500); Hot (8,000–50,000); and Intensely Hot (100,000 and above). In my experience, heat levels vary from batch to batch of peppers.

Below is a list of the chile peppers I like to cook with, in no particular order.

### Fresh Chile Peppers

From childhood, fresh chile peppers have been part of my daily diet. The most common in Mom's dishes were serrano, jalapeño, poblano, *güero*, and *chile piquin*, whether fresh, roasted, poached, or grilled. Roasting and grilling peppers brings out the richness of their flavors; when fresh, they can be blended with fresh or roasted tomatoes, tomatillos, onion, garlic, and herbs in warm salsas and sauces. Peppers can also make the meal — a simple bowl of pinto beans in broth garnished with sliced serrano peppers, chopped onion, cilantro, and a touch of lime is delicious!

### Fresh Chile Pepper Varieties

- **Anaheim**: 500–2,500; mild to medium heat; bright green; common in Mexican and Southwestern cooking
- **Bola**: 10,000–30,000; mildly hot to hot; round and red in color; in dry form, referred to as "rattle chile" and *cascabel*
- **Chilaca**: 1,000–2,500; mild to hot; dark green to dark brown/black in color
- **Fresno**: 2,500–10,000; medium to hot; red in color; somewhat fruity in flavor
- **Güero**, caribe: 5,000–15,000; mild to hot; pale yellow with a waxy skin
- **Habanero**: 100,000–350,000; intense heat; fruity and can come in a range of colors, including green, yellow, white, orange and red, brown and purple, depending on the variety
- **Jalapeño**: 2,500–8,000; mild to moderate heat; green when immature, red when mature
- **Manzano**: 12,000–30,000; hot, yellow orange in color; apple-shaped with black seeds
- **Piquin, chiltepin**: 40,000–58,000; hot; round or slightly elongated; green when immature, red when mature; also referred to as "bird pepper"
- **Poblano**: 1,000–2,000; mild to medium heat; dark green in color; native to Puebla
- **Serrano**: 10,000–23,000; sometimes intensely hot; green when immature, and yellow, orange, and red as it matures

## Dried Chile Peppers

Mexican dried chile pods are the dried version of some of the most popular fresh Mexican chile peppers. Each variety comes with its own distinct color—from vibrant red to almost black—and heat levels go from mild to intensely hot.

A quick toast on a hot *comal* (griddle) or a dip into hot oil brings out the true flavors of dried peppers, flavors that run from smoky to slightly sweet and nutty. Toasted peppers can also be ground into powder to yield a beautiful array of colors.

Rehydrated, the peppers blend well with garlic, onion, spices, and more, yielding some truly luxurious sauces, such as the iconic dish of Mexico, mole.

## Dried Chile Pepper Varieties

- **Ancho, Pasilla**: 1,000–2,000; dried ripe poblano; mild heat; reddish brown in color; notes of raisin; wide
- **Arbol**: 15,000–30,000; also known as "tree chile"; intense heat; bright red in color; small and skinny
- **California**: 2,500–5,000; moderate heat; dried Anaheim; bright red in color; slightly sweet and smoky; medium to long in length
- **Cascabel**: 1,500–2,500; also known as "rattle chile"; mildly spicy; reddish brown in color; round
- **Chipotle**: 2,500–10,000; also known as *chile meco*; hot; a large dried jalapeño; smoky in flavor; tan in color; medium length
- **Chipotles in adobo**: 2,500–8,000; smoked and dried jalapeño peppers preserved in a tomato adobo with vinegar and spices; mildly hot to hot; hints of sweetness; small to medium in length
- **Guajillo**: 2,500–5,000; moderate heat; red-reddish brown in color; smooth and shiny; short to medium to long in length
- **Japones**: 15,000–30,000; name means "Japanese," although not from Japan; intense heat; burnt red in color; small, elongated
- **Morita**: 15,000–35,000; also known as chipotle *morita*; hot; smokey and fruity in flavor; reddish brown to almost black in color; wrinkled skin; small
- **Mulato**: 1,000–1,500; dried ripe poblano; mild heat; dark brown to almost black in color; hints of chocolate, slightly smoky; wide
- **Negro**: 15,000–25,000; mildly hot to hot; also known as "pasilla"; almost black in color; hints of licorice; long and skinny
- **New Mexico**: 2,500–8,000; mildly hot to hot; bright red in color; earthy flavor, hints of cherry
- **Piquin/chiltepin**: 30,000–60,000; extremely hot, distinct in flavor; bright red to burnt red in color; very small; round or slightly elongated
- **Puya**: 5,000–8,000; also known as *pulla*; mildly hot to hot; reddish brown; fruity flavor; small

### Fresh vs. Dried

Here is a short list of common chile pepper names, fresh and dried:

- **Anaheim**: chile California
- **Bola**: *chile cascabel*
- **Chilaca**: *chile pasilla* or *chile negro*
- **De Arbol**: *chile de arbol*
- **Jalapeño**: chile chipotle or *morita*
- **Mirasol**: *chile guajillo*
- **Poblano**: *chile ancho*
- **Serrano**: *chile seco*

## Spices

Where would a Mexican kitchen be without a wide array of spices? It's important to note that because Mexico comprises many regions, how and which spices are used can vary considerably. Not every Mexican home cook will prepare mole, for instance, in the exact same way with the exact same ingredients and spices. That goes for many dishes, such as *salsa roja* for enchiladas, *birria de res*, tamales *de puerco*, and so on. I truly embrace the differences and try to learn from them.

To cumin or not to cumin? In my years of preparing Mexican dishes, *comino* (cumin) has always been a mainstay. I can say it is a bit more popular in the northern states of Mexico, like Monterrey, where my parents were from, than in other regions. It was always added in small amounts to *guisados* (stews) and homemade pork chorizo.

There is a misconception that if you add cumin to your dishes, it's Tex-Mex cooking. This couldn't be further from the truth. Cinnamon, cloves, cilantro, coriander, and more were introduced to Mexico by the Spanish conquistadors. Allspice, annatto or *achiote*, cumin, oregano, *epazote*, and chile peppers are spices and herbs used by the indigenous peoples in pre-Hispanic times.

- **Achiota paste**: *recado rojo*, a vibrant red paste from ground annatto seeds combined with spic-es and herbs
- **Allspice**: *pimienta dulce entera*
- **Bay leaves**: *hojas de laurel*
- **Black peppercorn**: *pimienta negra*
- **Cinnamon**: *canela*
- **Clove**: *clavo*
- **Coriander**: *semilla de cilantro*
- **Cumin**: *comino*
- **Epazote**: a fragrant herb native to Mexico, often used in beans and stews
- **Ginger**: *jengibre*
- **Granulated garlic**: *ajo en grano*
- **Marjoram**: *mejorana*
- **Mexican oregano**
- **Rosemary**: *romero*
- **Salt**: *sal*
- **Thyme**: *tomillo*

## NUTS AND SEEDS

The origins of the nuts and seeds essential in a wide variety of traditional Mexican dishes can be traced back to the ancient civilizations of Mesoamerica. Toasted or fried, when ground into a paste, they can be blended with softened dried chiles for sauces, salsas, and adobos. Not only do they add a nutty flavor, but they are also important as thickening agents in sauces such as mole and *pipián*.

Toasted sesame seeds adorn a plate of chicken mole that simmers for hours. Fresh pomegranate seeds pop with color when carefully placed on an almost-white *nogada* sauce ladled over a *chile relleno*. Have you ever enjoyed fresh guacamole garnished with toasted *pepitas* or pomegranate seeds? Or blended fried peanuts into a toasted *chile de arbol* salsa?

The flavor combinations are next-level amazing!

- **Almonds**: *almendras*
- **Dried fruits or raisins**: *pasas de uva*
- **Mexican chocolate**: true Mexican chocolate is made with minimal ingredients: sugar, cacao, cinnamon, and soy lecithin
- **Peanuts**: *cacahuates*
- **Pecans**: *nueces pecanes*
- **Pumpkin seeds**: *semillas de calabaza*
- **Sesame seeds**: *ajonjoli*
- **Walnuts**: *nuez castilla*

Seven thousand years ago, the diet in the region that now makes up modern-day Mexico centered on corn. The indigenous peoples developed staple foods such as corn, beans, squash, tomatoes, chilies, and cacao. The Spanish conquest of the Aztecs introduced wheat, rice, dairy, pork, beef, and spices.

The rich fertile soil and climate of Mexico is key to the year-round growth and harvest season. Just a few years ago, according to the US Department of Agriculture, 69 percent of the vegetables and 51 percent of the fresh fruits consumed in the United States were imported from Mexico. Fresh produce is key to authentic, traditional Mexican dishes. In general, many Americans who enjoy Mexican food don't realize how much produce is used in everyday dishes, salsa, and sauces — the students in my Mexican cooking classes were surprised to see the wide selection of produce used in a complete Mexican dinner.

# Tools in My Mexican Kitchen

**Every home cook and chef has their favorite kitchen tools that make cooking and prep go a lot smoother. Here are a few of my must-have tools to get those delicious salsas and dishes on the table!**

## POWER BLENDER

If you prepare a lot of salsa and sauces first on the list of necessary tools is a good blender. Ten years ago, I invested in a power blender, the Vitamix brand, and never looked back. For recipes that require straining the sauces, the power blender eliminates that step completely. Regular blenders and food processors will work, but you may need to blend longer and then strain the sauce through a fine-mesh sieve to achieve a smooth and silky sauce.

## MOLCAJETE

To experience the flavors of a traditional and authentic salsa you need a *molcajete*—a mortar and pestle carved from volcanic lava rock. Purchase one that holds at least 2 cups of liquid. Pulsing the salsa ingredients in a blender or food processor will give the salsa a similar finish, although the salsa will not be as glossy-looking as it is when made in a *molcajete*, nor will it have the light earthy flavor the dish imparts.

If you enjoy grinding your own spices in small quantities, a small *molcajete* works great! To cure the new dish, grind uncooked rice aggressively inside the bowl using the *tejolote* (pestle) until the surface feels smooth and polished. This may take 5 to 6 times, changing the rice out after each session. Use a strong brush with plenty of hot water to clean.

## ROLLING PIN

Speaking of tortillas, my favorite rolling pin is a 12-inch cherrywood pin with tapered ends. Traditional rolling pins with handles work as well. In a pinch, a wine bottle filled with beans and tightly sealed can serve as a rolling pin.

## TORTILLA PRESS

When it comes to corn tortillas, a metal press that is compact, heavy, and well-made makes the tortilla-making experience a lot easier. A wide variety of presses in all sizes is available from most Mexican markets and online. After much practice, I have learned to press an even tortilla in one press.

One time I forgot my press for a special dinner I was cooking for thirty people. I pressed a hundred corn tortillas using a plastic storage bag and a heavy cast-iron skillet. It worked!

## GRIDDLE (*COMAL*)

Choose a nonstick *comal* (griddle) for preparing corn tortillas. The flour tortillas are more forgiving, and a metal or cast-iron *comal* will work. You will have to temper the heat as you go. The all-metal Mexican griddles are fine, but they tend to burn hotter in the middle and can cook the tortillas unevenly. The metal *comal* is ideal for roasting, and for toasting salsa ingredients and dried chiles, nuts, seeds, and spices. And, of course, for reheating tortillas.

## TORTILLA WARMER

Keep tortillas warm and soft in a tortilla warmer made of cloth and insulated or in a small basket lined with a dish towel.

## POTS AND PANS

Let's get into it! You do not need fancy pots and pans to pull off the most delicious Mexican meals! I have tried so many different styles of cookware in the past. Low- and slow-cooking for the stovetop, I will pull out my cast-iron enamel Dutch oven pots. They are heavy and the heat is evenly distributed and they can go in the oven for long braising times.

In my collection of pots, you will also find the more traditional *ollas de peltre* (Mexican blue graniteware) and *ollas de barro* (Mexican clayware). My *abuelita* and *tias* cooked with them back in the day and I still use them in my kitchen today. The graniteware is lightweight and easy to clean. The clayware can be cured easily by soaking the new pieces in warm water for several hours. Fill with water three-quarters full and put over low heat. Bring to a light simmer and let the water cook down by half. Once dry, take fresh garlic and rub a light layer over the unglazed outside bottom of the pot. This creates a light seal. The clayware holds the heat well once it comes to temperature.

Stainless-steel skillets with tight lids are ideal for preparing the perfect Mexican rice and lots of *guisados* (stews and sautés). I do keep one or two nonstick skillets specifically for cooking egg dishes.

## COOKING UTENSILS AND CONTAINERS

- Wooden spoons, in all sizes, are my first choice for everyday cooking.
- A sturdy masher for beans is a must, but, in a pinch, you can use the bottom of a heavy mug.
- Silicone spatulas for when you really need to clean out a bowl, skillet, or blender jar, definitely!
- You also need bowls and storage containers, with lids, of all sizes to accommodate prepping ahead and leftovers.
- Glass mason jars are my favorite way to store homemade salsa in the refrigerator. Avoid plastic because it absorbs odors and the red chile will stain the plastic.
- A few other essential tools in my kitchen are a stand mixer, an electric handheld mixer, pressure cookers in two sizes (6 quart and 8 quart), a kitchen timer, digital meat thermometers, baking sheets with wire racks, 12- to 20-quart steamer pots, and airtight storage containers for dried chiles and spices.

Salsa Macha-
Tomatillo
chile de Arbol Salsa
Salsa de
Roasted Tomatillos
Salsa x 2
Salsa
Al Pastor Adobo
Salsa de Cacahuate
Salsa Negra
Smokey mortar
Jalapeño
Salsa

# Tips and Techniques

**I want to share with you some of my favorite tips and techniques for preparing delicious salsas, sauces, and adobos every time!**

## WHY COOK YOUR SALSA?

I'm asked this question all the time when I share my salsa-preparation videos. After experimenting with and developing salsa recipes for more than forty years, I've found that cooked salsa lasts longer in the refrigerator than salsas stored straight from the blender.

Have you ever made a tomato or tomatillo salsa, only to open it the next day and find it clumpy or separated? That's because tomatoes and tomatillos contain natural pectin. If you're partially roasting or poaching them, you may not be cooking them long enough to break down that pectin, which can lead to separation.

To avoid this, pour your blended salsa into a saucepan and bring it to a simmer for 10 minutes, stirring occasionally. Let it cool completely, then store it in glass mason jars in the refrigerator for up to 20 days.

Don't get me wrong — you can absolutely serve your salsa right after blending, especially if you're adding fresh cilantro and want its bright flavor to shine. Alternatively, you can cook the salsa, let it cool, and then gently blend it with fresh cilantro afterward. Another way to preserve salsa is to add 1 to 2 tablespoons of distilled white vinegar while it simmers.

Also, don't bring the whole jar of salsa to room temperature each time you serve it. Instead, pour out only what you'll use. Constant temperature changes can cause the salsa to spoil more quickly.

## COOKING METHODS

The traditional roasting method I learned from my mom was to heat a large cast-iron *comal* (griddle) over medium-high heat. The peppers were laid out evenly and slowly roasted, turned as needed. I can still vividly see, hear, and smell the aroma as the poblanos roasted.

Fire-roasting directly over an open flame is ideal if you have a gas stove or an outdoor grill. Just be aware that roasting times will vary. For *chiles rellenos*, for example, you don't want to overcook the peppers while roasting — they'll become too soft, and the flesh will tear more easily.

If your oven has a good broiler, this method is fast and almost foolproof. Choose peppers that are mostly flat and not curled, which helps ensure even blistering. Rub a light coat of oil on the peppers and place them on a baking sheet. Depending on your broiler, cooking times may vary. Position the peppers about 6 inches below the broiler, set to high, for 5 minutes. Then flip and broil for another 5 minutes. Once the skins are mostly blistered, transfer the peppers to a covered bowl or a plastic bag for 15 minutes. The steam will loosen the skins, making them easier to remove.

If you're going to use the peppers for a blended sauce or slice them into *rajas* (strips), here's a great tip: Before roasting, slice the bottoms off and carefully remove the seeds. This eliminates the messy step of seeding them later!

Dry roasting is the technique of roasting ingredients on the stovetop without oil. It's a common method for preparing salsa ingredients. A light drizzle of oil will speed things up, but slow roasting without oil brings out more flavor. It's important to learn the ideal cooking times for each ingredient: garlic (with skin on) will be ready in about 15 minutes; peppers will vary depending on their size and whether they're sliced open; tomatoes and tomatillos can take up to 25 minutes.

## PREVENTING A BITTER FLAVOR

Occasionally, a dried chile salsa or sauce may taste bitter, often due to old, brittle chile pods. In my experience, brittle and hard peppers yield bitter flavors. Keep dried chile pods stored in airtight containers in a cool spot; direct sunlight and heat will cause them to become brittle and fade in color.

When blending your salsa or sauce, discard the pepper-soaking water if it tastes bitter. I only use some of the cooking water when I know the pods are freshly dried. If your sauce is still bitter after cooking, mix in a bit of sugar. I personally enjoy pouring in a little vinegar and adjusting the salt, as the vinegar adds a pleasant touch of acidity. Let the sauce cook slowly to cook out any impurities and develop more flavor.

Part of the sour gooseberry family, the most common tomatillos found in markets are naturally very tart and may yield a sour salsa. Season accordingly when preparing salsa or sauce using these tomatillos. Cooking them thoroughly is important as well. The tomatillo called *milpero* is much smaller and is a mix of purple and green. This variation tends to be sweeter and less tart.

There are two schools of thought as to why a tomatillo salsa is bitter. One side says that you should not let the tomatillos tear open when cooking them. The other says that the salsa is sour because you didn't let them boil to the point of tearing open! This is when you need to get into your kitchen and test out a few recipes and find what works for you. I am on the side that says do not let the tomatillos tear open. Plus, when they tear open, you lose all that delicious pulp and the seeds from the plant end up floating in the cooking water.

## SERVING SALSA

If you're preparing salsa for a taco night, game night, or Mexican-themed dinner party, don't stress! Make the salsa the morning of your dinner and serve it when it's time. Enjoy it as fresh as possible.

From mild to extra spicy — we all have our heat preferences. A milder salsa is easy to achieve by simply adding fewer chile peppers and increasing the amount of tomato or tomatillo. In red salsa recipes that use dried peppers, eliminate some of the hotter ones — like *arbol*, *japones*, or *piquin* — and substitute with *guajillo* or California peppers.

Are you a chunky or smooth salsa lover? I enjoy both, depending on the mood. For a coarser salsa, use the pulse button on the blender to combine the ingredients. If the recipe includes softened dried chiles, blend those first with some water until mostly smooth before adding the other ingredients. For the smoothest salsa, a high-powered blender works best, but a regular blender works too — you may just need to blend on high a little longer. Don't overblend if you're using a power blender; you still want to see some of the seeds from the peppers, tomatoes, or tomatillos.

In my opinion, sauces and adobos taste even better after sitting for a couple of days as the flavors intensify! I used to freeze many of my red chile sauce and adobo recipes — they keep well for up to 6 months and still taste delicious.

# Salsa Fresca

## FRESH SALSA

Welcome to the heart of Mexican freshness, where vibrant flavors dance in every bite! *Salsa fresca*, or as many know it, *pico de gallo*, is where we begin — a celebration of ripe tomatoes, onions, chiles, and cilantro all coming together in their purest form.

But this is just the beginning of our fresh salsa journey. We'll be exploring the tangy kick of Tomatillo Serrano (page 32), the sweet heat of Cherry Tomato Chile Piquin (page 33), and even venturing into the tropical with Pineapple Habanero (page 26) and Mango Chipotle (page 28). As a little bonus, you'll learn how to use these salsas to elevate your favorite dishes like Slow Cooker Pork Carnitas (page 40), crispy Beef Taquitos (page 39), and perfectly Blackened Fish (page 37). So, get your cutting board ready, because we're about to dive into a world of fresh, flavorful salsas that will transform your meals!

# Salsa Mexicana

## PICO DE GALLO

Salsa Mexicana, also known as the popular *pico de gallo*, represents the colors of the Mexican flag. This was the first salsa recipe I learned to prepare when I was fourteen years old. It's made up of fresh Roma tomatoes, spicy and crisp serrano peppers, white onion, fragrant cilantro, fresh lime juice, and salt. My job on the weekends was to prepare a huge bowl of *pico de gallo* for my parents' taqueria. I remember Dad dragging me out of a sound sleep at five o'clock in the morning on Saturdays and Sundays to get to work. In hindsight, I am so thankful for those days!

This dish is best enjoyed fresh, but can be incorporated into many other recipes. Serve with freshly made chips or as a taco garnish.

PREP TIME: **25 MINUTES**

YIELD: **4 CUPS**

2 pounds (about 10 medium) Roma tomatoes, finely chopped

1 medium white onion, finely chopped

2 serrano peppers, finely chopped

Generous handful of fresh cilantro, minced

2 tablespoons fresh lime juice (1 large lime)

Salt and pepper, to taste

Combine all the ingredients and stir well. Cover and let the salsa sit for 30 minutes before serving.

TIPS & VARIATIONS

- **Garlicky Pico: Stir in 1 to 2 cloves of minced garlic and a drizzle of olive oil.**
- **Smoky Pico: Mix in 1 to 2 finely chopped chipotles in adobo.**
- **Chunky Guacamole: Mix in 3 large, mashed avocados.**
- **The fresh *pico* is a great addition to *frijoles charros*, seafood ceviche, and cactus (*nopales*) salad.**

# Pineapple Habanero Salsa

I truly enjoy the combination of fresh pineapple with habanero peppers! Growing up, I enjoyed my fair share of fresh fruits with spicy *chile de arbol* and lime. So, it makes sense that I would love spicy fruit salsa. Other fruits that pair well with hot peppers are mangos, peaches, strawberries, oranges, apricots, and green apples. Serve with homemade chips. This salsa is also delicious with pork chops or your favorite grilled chicken and seafood!

PREP TIME: **35 MINUTES**
YIELD: **3½ CUPS**

1 large pineapple (about 2 pounds)

2 habanero peppers

1 medium red onion, finely chopped

Large handful of fresh cilantro, minced

2 to 4 tablespoons fresh lime juice (1 to 2 large limes)

¼ cup agave syrup (optional)

2 teaspoons Tajín or your favorite chile-lime seasoning

Salt, to taste

Peel and finely dice half of the fresh pineapple and transfer to a bowl. Remove the pineapple from the remaining half. Reserve the fruit for another recipe or enjoy it fresh. Reserve half the hollowed-out pineapple and use it as a serving bowl for your salsa.

Carefully remove the stems and seeds from the habanero peppers, then finely dice them. To the bowl of pineapple, mix in the habanero, onion, cilantro, lime juice, agave, and Tajín. Season with salt. Cover and chill for 20 minutes.

When ready to serve, transfer the salsa from the bowl into the hollowed-out pineapple half.

TIPS & VARIATIONS

- **Fresh pineapple yields the best flavor, in my opinion, but in a pinch, you can use canned pineapple.**
- **Try this salsa on baked ham or on a spicy Hawaiian pizza — it's a tasty flavor combination!**
- **Grill the pineapple slices, habaneros, red onion, and 4 tomatillos. Combine all the chopped ingredients as instructed in the above recipe. The taste will be on a whole other level!**

# Mango Chipotle Salsa

I used to think that the only way to enjoy mango was on a stick with lots of lime juice, *chile limon* powder, and hot sauce! That truly was the only way I enjoyed fresh fruits as a kid. Little did I know that fresh mango makes for a delicious sweet, savory, and spicy salsa!

PREP TIME: **20 MINUTES**
YIELD: **4 CUPS**

2 large, fresh mangos (about 2 pounds total), peeled and chopped

3 chipotles in adobo, minced

1 large jalapeño pepper, minced

½ cup finely chopped red onion

⅓ cup fresh cilantro, minced

2 tablespoons fresh lime juice (1 large lime)

2 tablespoons honey or agave

2 teaspoons chile-lime powder seasoning

Salt and pepper, to taste

In a large glass bowl, combine all the ingredients. Stir well to combine. Taste for seasoning. Cover and let sit for 30 minutes before serving.

TIPS & VARIATIONS

- **Smoky chipotle, *morita*, and habanero peppers all pair very well when preparing fruit-based salsa.**
- **Add a large, roasted red pepper to the mango salsa — it will bring out more flavor without upping the heat.**
- **Fruit salsa pairs well with any seafood dish and is excellent on grilled chicken or pork chops.**

# Serrano Lime Salsa

Serrano lime salsa is literally ready in minutes! I have experimented with many variations of this salsa these past 35 years. Sometimes it is all fresh, sometimes cooked, roasted, grilled, smoked, or combination of fresh and grilled! You name it, I've tried it!

PREP TIME: **15 MINUTES**
YIELD: **3 CUPS**

8 ounces (about 14) serrano peppers, stemmed and coarsely chopped

¾ cup fresh lime juice (6 large limes)

¼ cup distilled white vinegar

Salt, to taste

Transfer the serrano peppers to a blender jar. Pour in the fresh lime juice, starting with the juice of 5 limes. Add the vinegar and ½ cup cold water. Use the pulse button to blend the salsa. If you prefer a less-chunky texture, blend on high — the consistency is up to you.

Once blended, taste for salt. If you want a stronger lime flavor, mix in the remaining lime juice. Store in the refrigerator for up to 10 days.

TIPS & VARIATIONS

- **This easy serrano salsa is inspired by the serrano salsa Mom prepared and served with *caldo de res* (beef soup).**
- **To create salsa that can be kept longer, cook it at a gentle simmer for 10 minutes after blending, then store in the refrigerator for up to 30 days.**
- **Mix with mayonnaise and shredded cabbage and serve as a garnish for fish or beer-battered shrimp tacos!**

# Tomatillo Avocado Salsa

As simple as this salsa sounds, it has always been one of my most requested recipes for the past thirty-eight years. My friends lovingly named it "the green sauce"! Fresh avocado, tart tomatillos, spicy serrano or jalapeño peppers, bright-white onion, cilantro, fresh lime juice, and salt! Mom prepared this must-have salsa for her famous beef *taquitos*. No home-cooked Mexican dinner would be complete without a big bowl of this creamy salsa, paired, of course, with a big bowl of homemade chips! If you want to further switch things up, mix in serrano, jalapeño, or *chile güero* peppers.

PREP TIME: **15 MINUTES**

YIELD: **2 CUPS**

12 ounces (about 6 large) tomatillos, husked and coarsely chopped

3 serrano peppers, stemmed and coarsely chopped

¼ medium white onion, chopped

2 large avocados

Handful of fresh cilantro

2 tablespoons fresh lime juice (1 large lime)

Salt, to taste

Combine all the ingredients plus ½ cup of cold water in a blender jar. Blend on high until smooth. Taste for salt. If the mixture is too thick, add a little more water. You can adjust the heat level in this salsa (or any other) by adding more or fewer peppers.

TIPS & VARIATIONS

- **Pure Avocado Salsa: Blend all the same ingredients, minus the tomatillos, plus an extra ½ cup of cold water. If needed, pour in a little more water to reach the desired consistency. This salsa comes out extra creamy!**
- **Roasted Avocado Salsa: On a preheated griddle over medium heat, add tomatillos, serrano peppers, onion, and 2 cloves chopped garlic. Drizzle with 1 teaspoon avocado oil. Turn ingredients as needed for 10 to 13 minutes until aromatic, sizzling, and lightly charred. Blend the roasted ingredients as instructed with the others; the flavors are amazing!**
- **Warm Avocado Salsa: Poach tomatillos, peppers, onion, garlic, and cilantro in 5 cups of water over medium heat. Once the tomatillos turn olive green, remove from the heat. Transfer ingredients to a blender, then add 1 large avocado and just enough cooking water to cover three-quarters of the ingredients. Season with salt to taste and blend on high until smooth. Pour into a saucepan, heat on low, and simmer for 10 minutes. Ladle generously over crispy rolled tacos for a delightful combination.**

# Tomato Serrano Salsa

Not always, but occasionally, I like to prepare salsa in a *molcajete*. The volcanic rock gives the salsa an earthy flavor and glossy finish that only a *molcajete* can provide. This *molcajete* tomato-serrano salsa couldn't be easier. If you enjoy a fresh salsa Mexicana (*pico de gallo*), you'll love this version. What's different about this *molcajete* salsa? I use a combination of roasted and fresh ingredients.

PREP TIME: **20 MINUTES**
COOK TIME: **25 MINUTES**
YIELD: **2 CUPS**

18 ounces (about 6 medium) Roma tomatoes

5 cloves garlic

½ teaspoons sea salt, plus more to taste

6 serrano peppers, stemmed and coarsely chopped

2 tablespoons fresh lime juice (1 large lime)

½ cup chopped onion

2 tablespoons fresh cilantro, minced

Core the tomatoes. On a preheated *comal* or griddle over medium heat, dry roast the tomatoes and garlic together. Turn as needed. Remove the garlic after 15 minutes and set aside. Continue roasting the tomatoes for a further 10 minutes.

Once the garlic cools, peel and transfer to the *molcajete*. Add the sea salt and grind into a paste.

Add the peppers to the garlic paste and continue grinding. Remove the skin from the tomatoes and grind them into the other ingredients. Add the lime juice, then salt to taste. Before serving, fold in the onion and fresh cilantro.

TIPS & VARIATIONS

- **Peeling the skins off the roasted tomatoes makes it easier to grind in the *molcajete*.**
- **You can roast the serrano peppers, but adding them fresh adds to that crisp, fresh salsa flavor.**
- **Soften 2 to 3 dried *chile morita* in simmering water for 10 minutes. Grind them with the garlic and peppers. They will add a smoky flavor and give the salsa a good bit of heat!**

# Beef Taquitos

Beef *taquitos*, flautas, and tacos *dorados* — I love them all! When I was young, shredding cooked beef for these classic dishes was not my favorite job, but I was able to taste-test as I went along, which made the task more enjoyable. When we prepared these at home, there was always a freshly blended Tomatillo Avocado Salsa (page 31) and a side of Mexican rice on hand. Serve with lettuce, crumbled Mexican cheese, and Mexican *crema*.

PREP TIME: **35 MINUTES**
COOK TIME: **1 HOUR, 35 MINUTES**
YIELD: **6 SERVINGS**

- 1½ pounds chuck roast
- 1½ teaspoons salt
- ½ medium onion
- 4 cloves garlic
- 2 bay leaves
- 18 corn tortillas (6-inch size)
- 2½ cups vegetable oil, for frying

In a medium pot, cover the chuck roast with water and add the salt, onion, garlic, and bay leaves. Bring to a simmer over medium heat. Continue cooking the beef until it shreds easily with two forks, about 1 hour. When it's ready, remove the beef from the water and shred it while the meat is still warm. Set aside.

Brush the tortillas lightly with oil on each side. Stack the tortillas and place them in a plastic storage bag. Fold the top of bag down, leaving it unsealed, and microwave on high for 1 minute.

Take 2 tablespoons of beef and fill the softened tortilla on the side closest to you. Roll as tightly as you can and set them seam-side down. Repeat until all the tortillas are filled. Using toothpicks, secure three *taquitos* together, seam sides touching, side by side. Pierce through with two toothpicks toward the center, spacing 1½ inches apart.

In a medium skillet, preheat the oil for 5 to 7 minutes over medium heat. Fry 5 to 6 *taquitos* at a time, but don't overcrowd the pan. Fry for a few minutes per side, or until golden and crispy.

Line a bowl with paper towels and transfer the *taquitos* into a standing position into the bowl to drain.

### TIPS & VARIATIONS

- ***Taquitos* can be prepared ahead of time and warmed in a preheated 350°F oven for 25 to 30 minutes. They are freezer-friendly as well.**
- **If using homemade corn tortillas, the best time to fill them is when the tortillas are still soft and warm. Place the filled *taquitos* seam-side down until ready to fry. There's no need to brush with oil or microwave. If using day-old tortillas, they will need the oil and microwave method.**

# Slow Cooker Pork Carnitas

Mention the word *carnitas* and it immediately transports me back to when my parents owned Blanca's Mexican Foods and the weekends were a popular time to enjoy *carnitas* with fresh *pico de gallo* salsa and fresh tortillas. This easy crockpot version of the dish comes together quickly and bypasses the fuss of deep frying!

**PREP TIME: 15 MINUTES**
**COOK TIME: 4 HOURS, 30 MINUTES**
**YIELD: 6 SERVINGS**

3½ pounds pork butt, cut into large chunks
2 teaspoons salt
2 teaspoons pepper
2 cups naturally rendered pork lard
1 large orange, sliced
10 cloves garlic
3 to 5 bay leaves
1½ teaspoons oregano
2 tablespoons fresh lime juice (1 large lime)
1-inch piece of cinnamon stick (optional)

Season the pork with the salt and pepper, then set aside. In the crockpot on high heat, add the naturally rendered pork lard.

Once the lard melts, turn the heat to low. Add all the ingredients in layers with the seasoned pork. Cover and cook on low for 4 hours.

After 4 hours, check the pork for tenderness. If it is tender, remove the pork from the crockpot and transfer it to a large skillet. Heat the *carnitas* over medium-high heat. Once the pork starts to sizzle and brown, drizzle in a little of the pork lard from the crockpot. Strain out the lard in the crockpot.

Turn the pork as needed until it reaches the desired browning and caramelization. Serve right away.

## TIPS & VARIATIONS

- **Boneless pork country ribs work great in this recipe in place of the pork butt.**
- **Use the leftover pork lard when preparing refried beans or making corn *masa* for tamales.**
- **Once the pork is tender, remove the orange and bay leaves. Drain out the excess fat. Pour in 4 cups of *chile ancho* sauce. Cook on low for another 60 minutes or until pork falls apart easily.**

# Salsa Guisada

## COOKED SALSA

Welcome to the world of cooked salsas, or *salsa guisada*, where the magic happens over heat, deepening flavors and creating rich, complex sauces. Here, we'll explore the smoky depths of roasted tomato poblano and roasted habanero, the bright tang of roasted tomatillo, and the warm, comforting notes of Chiltomate Salsa (page 47). Get ready to simmer, stir, and savor your way through these hearty salsas, perfect for everything from classic Huevos Rancheros (page 67) to creamy Enchiladas Suizas (page 66), and even to transform simple dishes like Nopalitos en Salsa (page 59) and Queso con Chile en Salsa (page 64) into something extraordinary.

# Spicy Jalapeño Salsa

This is as straightforward as it gets when it comes to a cooked salsa, and it's how I first learned to prepare a classic *salsa verde*. I still love this recipe to this day. Everything in the pot, boil, blend, season, and cook! You can choose your favorite cooking method, your favorite peppers, your favorite spices, and make this salsa your own.

**PREP TIME: 15 MINUTES**
**COOK TIME: 20 MINUTES**
**YIELD: 1 QUART**

12 ounces (about 6 large) tomatillos

10 ounces (about 6 extra-large) jalapeño peppers

¼ medium white onion

4 cloves garlic

Small bunch of fresh cilantro, stemmed

Salt, to taste

After removing the husk from the tomatillos and the stems from the jalapeños, rinse them under cool water. Transfer the tomatillos, peppers, onion, and garlic to a saucepan. Cover with water. Bring to a light boil over medium heat.

Once the mixture comes to a boil, reduce the heat slightly and continue cooking for 10 to 12 minutes, or until the tomatillos turn color most of the way. Remove the pot from the heat and let stand for 15 minutes.

Drain out three-quarters of the water from the salsa ingredients. Transfer everything to the blender and add the cilantro. Salt to taste. Blend on high until smooth, then transfer the blended salsa back to the saucepan and heat to medium. Once the salsa begins to simmer, stir as needed. It should be a light simmer, not a rapid boil. Continue cooking for 10 minutes. Taste for salt.

Once cool, pour the salsa into glass mason jars and seal tightly. Refrigerate for up to 10 days.

### TIPS & VARIATIONS

- **When cooking tomatillos in simmering water, you don't want them to tear open, only to change color. The thinking is that if they tear open, your salsa can taste bitter.**
- **Add 5 softened chile California to the mix before blending to yield a red version of this salsa recipe!**
- **This jalapeño salsa is excellent for *chilaquiles*, smothered burritos, tacos *ahogados*, *chicharrones*, and *nopales*.**

# Salsa de Mesa

This basic tomato salsa can be found on the table of most Mexican homes, where homestyle dishes are made daily. When I visited my *Tia* Minerva, Mom's younger sister, in Monterrey, she prepared this salsa almost twice a week. It was placed on the table for *la comida* (late lunch) and *la cena* (dinner).

**PREP TIME: 10 MINUTES**
**COOK TIME: 22 MINUTES**
**YIELD: 2 CUPS**

1½ pounds (about 7 medium) Roma tomatoes

2 to 4 serrano peppers, stemmed

¼ medium white onion

1 to 2 cloves garlic

Salt, to taste

1 tablespoon avocado oil

Slice an X on the bottom of the tomatoes, then transfer all the ingredients except the oil to a saucepan. Cover with 5 cups of water and bring the water to a boil over medium heat. Reduce the heat and continue cooking for 10 to 12 minutes, or until the tomato skins begin to pull away. If you want a stronger flavor of garlic, don't add it until you blend the salsa.

Transfer the tomatoes to a plate; once cool enough to handle, remove the skins.

Transfer the ingredients from the saucepan to a blender, including the juices left on the plate from the tomatoes. Add ½ cup of the cooking water. Season with salt. Blend until smooth.

Depending on how you like your salsa, you can blend on high until very smooth or pulse for a coarser finish.

In a saucepan, heat the oil to medium. After a few minutes, pour in the blended salsa. Reduce the heat slightly and continue cooking the salsa for 7 to 10 minutes. Taste for salt. Let cool before storing in an airtight container in the refrigerator for up to 12 days.

### TIPS & VARIATIONS

- **Removing the cores and skins from the tomatoes will yield a smoother salsa.**
- **Switch out the tomatoes for tomatillos to prepare an easy *salsa verde*. The only difference in the *salsa verde* recipe is you will add fresh cilantro when blending.**
- **This salsa recipe is a delicious tomato base for Mexican rice, *carne guisada*, and *caldo de pollo*. Serve it warm over *huevos rancheros*!**

# Chiltomate Salsa

*Chiltomate*? Chile and tomato together equals *chiltomate*! I enjoy all kinds of salsa, but I tend to favor the flavors of this zesty blend. I take my salsa-making seriously, as you can tell! If you are intimidated by habanero peppers, don't worry. I felt the same way, until I tried them for the first time and fell in love with the flavor. The heat wasn't nearly as bad as I'd feared — I've eaten serrano and jalapeño peppers with way more heat.

PREP TIME: **10 MINUTES**
COOK TIME: **35 MINUTES**
YIELD: **2 CUPS**

1 pound (about 5 medium) Roma tomatoes
2 habanero peppers, stemmed
⅓ medium white onion
2 cloves garlic, skin on
1 tablespoon avocado oil
2 tablespoons fresh lime juice (1 large lime)
Salt, to taste
Pinch of oregano

Wash the tomatoes and peppers, coring the tomatoes, then transfer them along with the onion and garlic to a griddle or skillet set over medium-low heat. For easy cleanup, line the griddle with aluminum foil before dry roasting the ingredients. Turn everything as needed for the next 20 to 25 minutes, removing the garlic after 15 minutes. Once the garlic is cool enough to handle, peel the cloves.

Transfer all the dry-roasted ingredients to a blender. Blend on high until smooth. Set aside.

In a saucepan, preheat the oil to medium heat for a few minutes. When the oil is hot, pour in the salsa from the blender. Reduce the heat slightly and continue cooking for 8 to 10 minutes. Remove from the heat and let cool.

Spoon however much salsa you want to enjoy right away and refrigerate the rest. Store the cooled salsa in lidded glass jars in the coldest part of the refrigerator. Avoid leaving the jars at room temperature, as this can cause spoilage. Cooked salsa lasts for 10 days in the refrigerator.

### TIPS & VARIATIONS

- **During the summer, I enjoy preparing this salsa with the yellow heirloom tomatoes from the farmers' market. They are slightly sweeter than Roma tomatoes.**
- **Substitute large tomatillos for the Roma tomatoes to creat a tangy, spicy *salsa verde*.**
- **Use a few extra tomatoes in the mixture and while the salsa is simmering, add your favorite seafood. Serve over linguini for a complete meal.**

# Tomatillo Chile de Arbol Salsa

Tomatillo *chile de arbol* salsa was a staple in our house growing up. My siblings and I could not enjoy a corn tortilla quesadilla or pork tamales without it. Every time I would fly home to visit my parents, there was always a big bowl of this freshly prepared salsa on the table.

Mom's version was simply to boil all the ingredients together and then blend. There's something to be said for the simplicity of that!

PREP TIME: **10 MINUTES**
COOK TIME: **15 MINUTES**
YIELD: **2 CUPS**

1 pound (about 11 medium) tomatillos

6 dried *chile de arbol*, stemmed

2 serrano peppers, stemmed

¼ medium white onion

3 cloves garlic

Small handful of fresh cilantro

Salt, to taste

After peeling and washing the tomatillos, transfer them to a pot and cover them with water. Add the *chile de arbol*, serrano peppers, onion, and garlic. Bring everything to a boil, reduce to a simmer, and cook for 10 minutes. Remove from the heat.

Using a slotted spoon, transfer the ingredients to the blender jar. Pour in ½ cup of the cooking water and the cilantro. Season to taste with salt. Pulse at medium-high speed until the salsa is mostly smooth and you can still see the red chile flakes. Taste for salt.

You can serve the salsa as is. It will yield a bright-green salsa with flakes of cilantro and *chile de arbol*. Or you can transfer the blended salsa to a saucepan and heat to medium. When it comes up to a simmer, reduce heat slightly and continue cooking for 7 to 10 minutes. The color of the salsa will darken slightly. Cooking the salsa cooks out the natural pectin and produces a smooth salsa that will last up to 10 days when refrigerated.

TIPS & VARIATIONS

- **Most tomatillos found are the larger all-green ones. You can find the tomatillo *milpero* in many Mexican markets. These are much smaller and come in shades of purple and green combined. They yield a slightly sweeter salsa.**
- **With some added stock, this recipe can be used for slow-simmered beef or pork. It's excellent for a quick chicharron, eggs, *panela* cheese, or *nopales* (cactus) *en salsa*.**

# Salsa Ahumada

## SMOKED SALSA

If you could have seen my face the first time I tasted smoked salsa! Just when I thought I had tried about every salsa known to man, I tasted this! It was during a trip to Austin, Texas, while visiting my brother, Ismael, and his wife, Janet Lynn. The love of cooking and good home-cooked meals rubbed off onto my brother as well, and he loves to grill and smoke all kinds of dishes. These smoked salsas are excellent on any of your favorite grilled meats, chicken, and fish, as well as roasted vegetables and baked potatoes!

PREP TIME: **25 MINUTES**
COOK TIME: **1 HOUR, 20 MINUTES**
YIELD: **5 CUPS EACH VERSION**

**SMOKIN' SALSA ROJA**

1½ pounds (about 7 medium) Roma tomatoes

4 red jalapeño or Fresno peppers, stemmed

2 green jalapeño peppers, stemmed

½ large white onion

4 cloves garlic, skin on

2 tablespoons fresh lime juice (1 large lime)

Salt, to taste

**SMOKIN' SALSA VERDE**

1 pound (about 11 medium) tomatillos

6 serrano peppers, stemmed

2 poblano peppers, stemmed

½ large white onion

4 cloves garlic, skin on

2 tablespoons fresh lime juice (1 large lime)

Salt, to taste

Medium handful of fresh cilantro

**YOU WILL NEED**

3 cups hickory chips, previously soaked in water

Charcoal

Outdoor grill

TIPS & VARIATIONS

- **Red jalapeño peppers, serranos, and even poblanos can be found in some Mexican markets or in supermarkets that carry a large assortment of Mexican produce. As the weather gets colder, some farmers' markets will also carry them. In a pinch, substitute fresh hot cherry peppers for the red jalapeños.**
- **I like to process or blend, by pulsing, all my veggies separately. I find that by doing this, I avoid big chunks of tomato or onion left behind. But if you like your salsa smoother, you can process or blend all together.**

Wash all the vegetables and place them in a metal dish lined with aluminum foil. Make sure the pan will fit on one side of the grill when the lid is closed.

Build your charcoal fire on one side of the grill. Preheat the coals until you reach 270°F to 300°F. Drain the hickory woods chips and place them on one side of the hot coals, in the center of grill. Once the chips start smoking, add the pan of vegetables to the indirect heat and cook for 30 minutes with the lid closed.

Turn all the vegetables over and move pan to the direct heat and continue cooking for another 30 minutes, or until the tomatoes and tomatillos are soft. You want most of the skin on the peppers to blacken and blister. Keep the grill lid closed as much as possible.

Before finishing the salsa recipes, remove the skin from the garlic and the skin and seeds from the poblano peppers. If using Fresno peppers, remove the skin; I leave the seeds for extra heat. The other chile peppers will be fine as is because the skin is thin.

For the *salsa roja*: In a food processor or blender jar, add the tomatoes, all the red and green jalapeño peppers, onion, garlic, lime juice, and salt. Pulse for a coarse salsa or blend on high for a smoother texture.

For the *salsa verde*: In a food processor or blender jar, add the tomatillos, poblanos, serranos, onion, garlic, lime juice, salt, and cilantro. Pulse for a coarse salsa or blend on high for a smoother texture.

If the salsas are too thick, mix in a little water to thin them. Serve warm or at room temperature. Cool completely and store in airtight containers in the coldest part of your refrigerator for up to 6 days.

# Creamy Taqueria-Style Salsa

What's the hardest part about preparing taqueria-style salsa? It's deciding which chile peppers to use. I tend to favor serrano chile peppers for the flavor and heat, but red jalapeño peppers are a close second! This salsa is delicious with tacos, grilled meats, or as a vibrant dip with tortilla chips.

PREP TIME: **7 MINUTES**
COOK TIME: **15 MINUTES**
YIELD: **2 CUPS**

8 ounces (about 14 medium) serrano peppers, stemmed and coarsely chopped

4 cloves garlic

¼ small white onion

1½ cups avocado oil, plus more as needed

2 tablespoons fresh lime juice (1 large lime)

Small handful of fresh cilantro

Salt, to taste

In a skillet over medium heat, add the peppers, garlic, onion, and oil. After a few minutes, the oil will begin to lightly fry and the ingredients will become aromatic. Take care that the heat isn't too high; you want the ingredients to simmer lightly for 10 minutes. Remove from the heat and let cool.

Using a slotted spoon, spoon the peppers, garlic, and onion into a blender jar, leaving the oil in the skillet. Add the lime juice, cilantro, and salt, to taste. Blend on high for 1 minute.

Cool the oil slightly and transfer it to a measuring cup for easy pouring. Blend the salsa on high speed, slowly adding the cooled oil until extra creamy and emulsified. Add more cooled oil if too thick, avoiding rapid addition to prevent separation.

Serve immediately or chill for later.

### TIPS & VARIATIONS

- **Before you begin any salsa recipe, make it a habit to wash the chile peppers and cilantro, if using, letting them dry completely.**
- **Change the flavor profile of any taqueria-style salsa by combining a variety of fresh peppers. Green with green and red with red, of course. For the green, you can also incorporate tomatillos, sliced open before frying.**
- **You don't need to just use fresh red chile peppers — you can combine dried red chiles with Roma tomatoes to yield a creamy fiery-orange salsa.**

# Roasted Tomatillo Salsa

Dry roasting ingredients is a traditional Mexican cooking method used to enhance the flavor of the salsa. It also makes this *salsa verde* look so appealing. I do lightly boil my salsa ingredients on occasion, but this roasted flavor is delicious and worth the effort. In a pinch, you can also broil the ingredients, although the end result will be slightly different.

PREP TIME: **15 MINUTES**
COOK TIME: **25 MINUTES**
YIELD: **3 CUPS**

2 pounds (about 10) tomatillos

5 serrano peppers

⅓ large white onion, thinly sliced

4 cloves garlic, skin on

Small bunch of fresh cilantro

Salt, to taste

Wash and peel the tomatillos. Transfer them to a cast-iron griddle. Add the serrano peppers, washed, and the onion and garlic. Heat to medium.

Flip and turn the ingredients as they begin to blister and blacken. I typically remove the garlic after 15 minutes, so it doesn't burn, although total cook time is 25 minutes. Take the griddle off the heat and let the ingredients cool for 15 minutes.

Peel the garlic and remove the stems from the serrano peppers. Transfer the tomatillos, peppers, onion, and garlic to the blender. Add the cilantro and 1 cup of water. Blend on high until smooth. Taste for salt.

TIPS & VARIATIONS

- **To extend the refrigerator life of your cooked salsa, after blending it, cook it at a simmer for 10 minutes. This will cook out the natural pectin and yield a smoother salsa that doesn't clump or separate when refrigerated.**
- **Blend 1 cup of Mexican *crema* with 2 cups of roasted *salsa verde* for a delicious, creamy enchilada sauce!**

# Tomato Chile de Arbol Salsa

What comes to mind when you hear *chile de arbol*? For me, it's red-hot spicy goodness! Without a doubt, I'm a chile-head and enjoy spicy salsa. If it's not spicy, then it tastes bland to me, so I sometimes fail when it comes to preparing a mild salsa. If you do want to reduce the heat level of any salsa recipe, simply add fewer chile peppers or bump up the number of tomato or tomatillo used.

**PREP TIME: 10 MINUTES**
**COOK TIME: 15 MINUTES**
**YIELD: 1½ CUPS**

12 dried *chile de arbol*, stemmed

2 serrano chile peppers, stemmed

2 cloves garlic, skin on

1 teaspoon avocado oil

8 ounces (about 2 large) Roma tomatoes

Salt, to taste

With the heat set to medium, transfer the *chile de arbol*, serrano peppers, and garlic to a griddle pan or skillet.

After 1 to 2 minutes, drizzle the oil onto the salsa ingredients. Next, core the tomatoes. Place the tomatoes in 4 cups of simmering water over medium heat. Cook until the skins pull away.

The ingredients on the griddle should become aromatic and sizzle a little. Toss them gently, as needed, until the dried *chile de arbol* begin to blacken. If the chiles start to smoke, the heat is too high!

Remove the dried chiles once you see blackening. Leave the serrano peppers until the skin blisters and blackens in spots. Remove the garlic after 15 minutes. Remove the skin from the garlic.

Transfer the chiles, garlic, and tomatoes to a blender. Pour ½ cup of the cooking water from tomatoes into the blender. Blend on high until the mixture is very smooth. Season with salt. Pour the blended salsa into a medium pot. Bring to a simmer and cook for 7 minutes. Serve the salsa warm or at room temperature.

Cool completely and store in a glass jar refrigerated for up to 10 days.

### TIPS & VARIATIONS

- **Why do I cook salsa after blending it? Cooking tomatoes or tomatillos helps remove the natural pectin they contain. Pectin is what makes your salsa clumpy or can cause it to separate when refrigerated. Cooking also improves the flavor and extends the life of the salsa.**
- **Soften 6 *chile guajillo*. Add them to the blender along with the rest of the ingredients, as well as 1 teaspoon cumin and 1 teaspoon oregano. Blend on high until smooth. You may need to mix in a little more water if the mixture is too thick. Cook as instructed. This sauce is excellent for spicy enchiladas, *chilaquiles*, and *huevos ahogados* (drowned eggs).**

# Toasted Chile de Arbol Tomatillo Salsa

Toasted *chile de arbol* combined with dry-roasted tomatillos is one of my favorite salsas! There are so many variations of tomatillo salsa to be prepared and enjoyed! Think outside the box when you approach a salsa recipe: combine fresh chile peppers with dried chile pods and mix tomatillos with tomatoes to add extra levels of flavor.

PREP TIME: **20 MINUTES**
COOK TIME: **30 MINUTES**
YIELD: **1½ CUPS**

12 dried *chile de arbol*, stemmed

12 ounces (about 9 medium) tomatillos, husked

2 serrano peppers, stemmed

1 teaspoon avocado oil

4 cloves garlic, skin on

Salt, to taste

Preheat a griddle over medium heat. Add the *chile de arbol*.

In the meantime, fill a saucepan with 1 cup of water and bring to a simmer over low heat. As soon as the *chile de arbol* become aromatic and begin to blacken, turn them quickly and leave for just a few seconds more. Transfer them to the saucepan of simmering water.

Add the tomatillos, serrano peppers, and garlic to a griddle set over medium heat. Drizzle with the oil. Using tongs, move the ingredients around to coat them in the oil. Roast for 15 minutes, then remove the griddle from the heat and cover it with aluminum foil for 10 minutes. The steam created will finish the cooking process.

When ready to blend the ingredients, remove the skins from the garlic. Reserve the water in the saucepan.

In a blender jar or food processor, add the *chile de arbol*, tomatillos, serrano peppers, garlic, ½ cup of the reserved cooking water, and salt, to taste. Blend on high for 45 to 60 seconds. If the salsa is too thick, pour in a little more cooking water until you achieve the desired consistency.

Store the salsa in lidded glass jars in the refrigerator for 5 to 6 days.

TIPS & VARIATIONS

- **Toasting the *chile de arbol* will add a smoky toasted flavor to the salsa, which is different from the taste you get when boiling the peppers.**
- **For a red salsa, use Roma tomatoes instead of tomatillos.**
- **If you like a tangy flavor, toast 2 chile California with the *arbol* peppers for a more intense red salsa.**
- **I especially enjoy serving this salsa with beef-cheek or beef-tongue tacos. It is common to fold in finely chopped onion and cilantro before serving.**

# Salsa Borracha

*Salsa borracha* translates to "drunken salsa." Traditional ingredients, such as fresh chile peppers, dried chile pods, tomato, tomatillo, onion, and garlic, are all part of the mix. The twist is the addition of Mexican beer. The flavors of the beer are subtle and pair well with any of your favorite grilled or pan-seared steaks.

PREP TIME: **15 MINUTES**
COOK TIME: **50 MINUTES**
YIELD: **1 QUART**

- 9 ounces (about 4 large) tomatillos, husked
- 9 ounces (about 3 large) Roma tomatoes
- 3 jalapeño peppers, stemmed
- 3 serrano peppers, stemmed
- ⅓ medium white onion
- 5 cloves garlic, skin on
- Salt, to taste
- 2 *chile ancho* pods, seeded, stemmed, and torn into small pieces
- 3 teaspoons avocado oil
- 12 ounces Mexican lager-style beer

In an extra-large skillet or *comal* (griddle) that has been preheated at medium, add the tomatillos, tomatoes, jalapeños and serrano peppers, onion, and garlic. If you don't have enough room, you can use two separate skillets.

Dry roast for 15 to 25 minutes. Remove the garlic, peppers, and tomatillos after 15 minutes. Continue roasting tomatoes for another 10 minutes, turning as needed.

When ready, transfer all the dry-roasted ingredients to a blender, peeling the garlic before adding it. Season with salt. Pulse to blend until you have a coarse-looking salsa. Set aside.

In a skillet over medium heat, add the torn pieces of *chile ancho*. Drizzle in the oil. Stirring often, fry the *chile ancho* for a few minutes, or until it becomes aromatic and toasty-looking.

Combine the coarse salsa and *chile ancho* in a skillet. Stir, cook for a few minutes, then add the beer. Once simmering, reduce the heat, taste for salt, and continue cooking until the *chile ancho* breaks down and the salsa thickens and darkens.

Cool and store airtight. Due to beer content, consume within 3 days.

## TIPS & VARIATIONS

- **Too many dried chiles? Make fresh-ground powder with an inexpensive coffee grinder. Destem, deseed, and lightly toast peppers for 1 minute. Tear, grind fine, and store in refrigerated freezer bags. Rehydrate with boiling water and combine with other spices for a beautiful sauce.**
- **This salsa recipe works with tequila or mezcal instead of beer. *Molcajete*-made, mostly dried chile versions are best fresh over hot grilled carne asada and only last a few days.**

# Nopalitos en Salsa

*Nopalitos en salsa* means "cactus in a warm salsa." In Mexico, it is very common to prepare cactus in many ways during Lent. Most often, the salsa is prepared with a combination of red dried chiles and tomatoes or tomatillos. You are not limited to just red salsa though; *salsa verde* is a popular option as well. Serve with pinto or black beans, whole or refried, and warm corn tortillas.

PREP TIME: **15 MINUTES**
COOK TIME: **40 MINUTES**
YIELD: **4 SERVINGS**

2 pounds (about 12) fresh cactus paddles, cleaned and chopped

½ teaspoon salt, plus more to taste

¼ medium white onion, coarsely chopped

4 cloves garlic, smashed

2 serrano peppers, sliced open

Small handful of fresh cilantro

2 cups Salsa de Mesa (page 46), Roasted Tomatillo Salsa (page 54), or Chile Cascabel Salsa (page 81)

To cook freshly chopped raw cactus, simply place them in a saucepan with the salt, onion, garlic, serrano peppers, and cilantro. Heat them over medium-low heat. After several minutes, they will begin to release their own liquid. Cook, stirring now and then, until most of the liquid has evaporated.

At this point, remove the onion, garlic, serrano peppers, and cilantro and discard. You can rinse the cactus or you can add your prepared salsa at this time. Taste for salt, let the mixture come up to a simmer, and cook gently for 10 minutes.

TIPS & VARIATIONS

- **Cleaned cactus paddles can be wrapped in plastic wrap and then placed in a heavy storage bag. Store in the freezer for several months. Pull out the paddles as you need them for your recipes.**
- **To bump up the servings, Mom would occasionally fold in 1 pound of previously chopped russet potatoes that had been fried.**
- **Switch out the tomato-based salsa for a pure *chile ancho* sauce with seared pork or beef ribs. Fold in the cooked cactus once the meat is tender.**

# Salsa de Habanero con Vinagre

Many people find habanero peppers to be a bit intimidating, but I absolutely love them! They pair well with all kinds of fruits, including pineapple, mango, and peach. This recipe includes a dose of vinegar, which may seem like an odd addition to salsa. But in Mexico, salsa is salsa, vinegar or no vinegar. This salsa is not really a chip-and-dip salsa, but more of a delicious garnish for other dishes. And a little goes a long way!

PREP TIME: **20 MINUTES**
COOK TIME: **28 MINUTES**
YIELD: **1½ CUPS**

1 medium carrot, peeled and sliced

7 ounces (about 14 large) habanero peppers, stemmed

6 cloves garlic, skin on

¼ small white onion

1 teaspoon avocado oil

½ cup distilled white vinegar

Salt, to taste

Place the carrot in a saucepan of simmering water. Cook for 10 minutes, or until tender. Set aside.

In the meantime, place the habaneros, garlic, and onion on a griddle or in a skillet over medium heat. Once the ingredients begin to roast and blacken, drizzle the oil over them. Toss to coat evenly. Cook for 6 to 8 minutes more. Let the garlic cool, then remove the skins.

In the blender jar, combine the carrot, habaneros, garlic, onion, vinegar, and ¾ cup of water. Season with salt. Blend on high until smooth, then transfer the mixture to a saucepan. Cook at medium heat for 8 to 10 minutes.

Cool to room temperature, then store in glass bottles in the refrigerator for up to 6 months.

TIPS & VARIATIONS

- **Take any fresh chile pepper, such as jalapeño, serrano, red jalapeño, red serrano, Fresno, *güero*, *piquin*, or Manzano, and use this same recipe to prepare a whole range of salsa varieties.**
- **The cooked carrots add a light touch of sweetness, but not enough to dramatically change the flavor of the salsa. The blended carrots also bring body to the mix.**

# Creamy No-Avocado Salsa

Creamy *salsa verde* with no avocado? How can that be? Not too long ago, the price of avocados went up so much in Mexico that people could not afford them. Imagine you sell tacos for a living and avocado salsa is a favorite of your customers? You've got no other choice than to find a work-around — enter this no-avocado salsa, a recipe born out of necessity. Delicious on tacos *dorados* and quesadillas, it makes a great dipping sauce for fresh vegetables, chicken strips, chips, and bacon-wrapped shrimp!

PREP TIME: **10 MINUTES**
COOK TIME: **12 MINUTES**
YIELD: **2 CUPS**

¼ cup avocado oil or extra-virgin olive oil

3 jalapeño peppers, sliced open

3 cloves garlic, smashed

¼ medium white onion, sliced

12 ounces (about 6 large) tomatillos, husked

6 ounces Mexican squash or zucchini, sliced into chunks (1 medium squash)

Medium handful of fresh cilantro

Salt, to taste

Add the oil, jalapeños, garlic, and onion. Heat to medium. Stir until the ingredients begin to sizzle and become aromatic. Cook for 7 to 8 minutes. Remove from the heat.

While the other ingredients are cooking, add the tomatillos and the squash to another pot. Cover with water and bring to a boil. When the water begins to simmer, set the timer for 8 minutes. Cook just until the tomatillos begin to turn from bright green to opaque green. Remove from the heat and let stand for 10 minutes.

Drain the water from the tomatillos and squash and transfer them to a blender. Add the peppers, garlic, onion, and the oil remaining in the skillet. Add the cilantro. Blend on high until smooth. Season with salt. If the salsa is too thick, pour in a little water and blend again.

This salsa will last up to 6 days in the refrigerator, although it's best eaten fresh.

### TIPS & VARIATIONS

- **This salsa became popular when the *taqueros* could not afford to prepare gallons of creamy avocado salsa every day. Did the patrons know they were not being served avocado salsa? Good question. The salsa is dang good is all I have to say!**
- **Because there is no avocado in this salsa, it can double as a creamy enchilada sauce or can be tossed with pasta and seafood.**

# Spicy Birria Salsa

Savory Mexican dishes go hand in hand with spicy salsa, which is typically served on the side or available on the table. This is my spicy salsa recipe. It can add heat to *birria*, and, yes, it pairs well with most of your favorite Mexican dishes.

**PREP TIME: 20 MINUTES**
**COOK TIME: 15 MINUTES**
**YIELD: 4½ CUPS**

1 pound (about 11 medium) tomatillos

2 cups dried *chile de arbol*

2 teaspoons olive oil

6 cloves garlic

¼ cup distilled white vinegar

Salt, to taste

Rinse and peel the tomatillos, then place them in a medium pot. Cover with 4 cups of water and bring to a boil. Reduce the heat and continue cooking until the tomatillos turn from bright green to an opaque-green color. Remove from the heat and let stand for 20 minutes.

In a skillet, add the *chile de arbol* and oil and heat to medium. After 1 minute or so, the chiles will begin to sizzle and become aromatic. Toss the chiles in the skillet for 1 to 2 minutes, then add 2 cups of water. Simmer for 10 minutes, then remove from the heat.

When ready, add the *chile de arbol* and water to the blender. Drain the water from the tomatillos and transfer them to the blender. Add the garlic, vinegar, and salt, to taste. Blend at the highest speed until smooth.

Store in airtight glass jars in the refrigerator for up to 2 months.

## TIPS & VARIATIONS

- **The vinegar in this recipe is optional, although I like the touch of acidity it brings. The vinegar also helps preserve the salsa a little bit longer.**
- **To yield a milder version of this salsa, eliminate ¼ cup of *chile de arbol* and substitute with *chile guajillo* peppers. Remove the stems and seeds from the *guajillo* peppers, tear them into pieces, and cook as instructed.**

# Queso con Chile en Salsa

*Queso con chile* or *chile con queso*? Either way, it's one of the most simple and delicious recipes around, consisting of freshly blended tomatoes with fresh serrano peppers and *panela* Mexican cheese. It's a homestyle and traditional dish prepared in a variety of ways, and it's delicious with avocado slices, refried beans, and warm tortillas.

A semisoft cow's milk cheese is perfect here because it has a low melting point. You want a cheese that can stand up to the warm salsa and be scooped up to enjoy with tortillas, chips, or *bolillos* (Mexican bread). This is one of my Top 5 Favorites of Mom's recipes.

PREP TIME: **20 MINUTES**
COOK TIME: **25 MINUTES**
YIELD: **4 SERVINGS**

4 serrano peppers, stemmed

1 large poblano pepper, seeded and stemmed

2 tablespoons avocado or extra-virgin olive oil

½ cup thinly sliced white onion

9 ounces (about 3 large) Roma tomatoes, coarsely chopped

2 cloves garlic

Pinch of oregano

Salt and pepper, to taste

12 ounces Mexican *panela* cheese, cubed

Place 2 of the serrano peppers and the poblano pepper on a sheet pan. Reserve the remaining 2 serrano peppers. Place the pan under a preheated broiler set at high for 10 minutes. Flip the peppers halfway through cooking time. When ready, transfer them to a plastic bag. Set aside.

In a large skillet over medium heat, preheat the oil for 3 minutes. Add the onion and cook for 5 minutes.

Coarsely chop the remaining 2 serrano peppers. In a blender jar, add the chopped peppers, tomatoes, garlic, oregano, ½ cup of water, and salt and pepper. Blend on high until smooth. Taste again for salt.

When ready, pour the blended tomato sauce into a skillet. Cook for 8 to 10 minutes, or until the sauce darkens and thickens.

Take the peppers out of the plastic bag. Remove the blistered skins, then slice the skinned peppers into thin strips. If you like, you can remove the seeds from the serrano peppers. Add the *rajas* (strips) to the simmering salsa. Cook for 3 minutes.

After 3 minutes, fold in the cubed *queso panela*. Stir to cover the cheese in the salsa. Cook for 2 minutes more.

Serve right away or turn the heat to the lowest setting and keep warm.

TIPS & VARIATIONS

- The beauty of recipes like this is that they can be prepared with any blended salsa. If the ingredients are blended raw, just give the salsa some time to cook before adding the cheese.
- If you want to kick up the flavors of this traditional recipe, try the *salsa asada* recipe blended to a coarse finish for the salsa base. Amazing!
- On occasion, Mom would serve toasted *bolillo* bread with this dish — it makes for a delicious meatless meal.

# Enchiladas Suizas

Enchiladas Suizas, tacos *al pastor*, and tacos *arabe* are just a few of the popular and traditional Mexican dishes that were influenced by the people who immigrated to the country. *Suizas* means "Swiss," and it was Swiss immigrants who brought their tradition of cooking with cheese and cream to Mexico.

PREP TIME: **35 MINUTES**
COOK TIME: **1 HOUR, 10 MINUTES**
YIELD: **4 SERVINGS**

4 cups previously cooked rotisserie chicken, shredded

2½ cups Roasted Tomatillo Salsa (page 54)

Salt and pepper, to taste

1½ cups Mexican *crema*

12 corn tortillas

¾ cup vegetable oil

8 ounces Chihuahua, Oaxaca, or Jack cheese, shredded

⅓ cup finely chopped cilantro

½ cup thinly sliced red onion

In a bowl, combine the shredded chicken with ½ cup of the salsa. Season lightly with salt and pepper. Reserve covered.

Transfer the remaining 2 cups of salsa to a saucepan and heat to medium. When the salsa begins to boil, reduce the heat and whisk in ¾ cup of the *crema*, reserving the rest for later. Cook for 1 minute more. Season with salt and pepper. Cover and set it aside.

In a skillet, preheat the oil to medium for 3 to 4 minutes. When oil is hot, flash fry the corn tortillas, until soft, for 20 seconds per side. Transfer to a plate lined with a paper towel and partially cover with foil.

Preheat the oven to 350°F.

Strain out the solids from the cooked chicken.

To the bottom of a 13-by-9-inch baking dish, spoon a very light layer of the reserved creamy salsa. Fill the tortillas with chicken. Roll tightly, and place them seam side down in the baking dish. Ladle the rest of the salsa over the top of the enchiladas. Top with the shredded cheese.

Place the baking dish on the middle rack of the oven. Bake for 25 minutes or until warmed through and the cheese has melted.

Serve 3 enchiladas per plate. Garnish with the reserved *crema*, chopped cilantro, and red onions.

TIPS & VARIATIONS

- **Prepare 2 days ahead by storing filled and rolled fried tortillas side by side in an airtight storage container. The next day, prepare the sauce. Assemble and bake the enchiladas on the third day.**

# Huevos Rancheros

Fried corn tortillas with fried eggs on top served with plenty of warm salsa — the classic *huevos rancheros*. My favorite version of the dish is a simple tomato salsa (*salsa de mesa*) warmed and poured over the top of the eggs. A fresh garnish of avocado and Mexican cheese completes the meal. Serve with beans.

**PREP TIME: 10 MINUTES**
**COOK TIME: 15 MINUTES**
**YIELD: 1 SERVING**

2 tablespoons avocado oil

2 corn tortillas

2 large eggs

Salt and pepper, to taste

⅓ cup of your favorite warm salsa (see Tips & Variations)

4 avocado slices

2 ounces *queso fresco* or *panela* cheese

Small handful of fresh cilantro, minced

In a nonstick skillet, preheat the oil to medium heat. After a few minutes, add the corn tortillas overlapping each other. Let them fry for 3 to 4 minutes per side, or until they begin to crisp up.

Once the tortillas are slightly crispy, gently add eggs toward the center of the overlapped tortillas. Season lightly with salt and pepper. Cover the skillet with a lid to finish cooking eggs to desired doneness. All stovetops will vary as far as cooking times, so just watch them for the next 5 minutes. You can add 1 tablespoon of water to the pan to help the eggs cook a little faster.

Once the eggs are cooked to your liking, transfer the *huevos rancheros* to a serving plate. Quickly add salsa to the hot skillet and cook until just warm. Pour the salsa over the eggs. Garnish with the avocado, cheese, and cilantro.

TIPS & VARIATIONS

- **A more traditional cooking method is to add the uncooked corn tortillas to a skillet with ½ cup of preheated oil. Add the uncooked eggs on top of the tortillas. Carefully spoon the oil over the tops of eggs until they are cooked to desired doneness.**
- **Almost any cooked salsa that is warmed works best for *huevos rancheros*. You can add a light layer of refried beans to the tortillas once they are slightly crisp and then add the eggs.**
- **Fry the corn tortillas ahead of time and set them aside. Fry equal the same number of sunny-side-up eggs or eggs over-easy as you have tostadas. When ready, spread a layer of refried beans over the tostadas. Place 2 tostadas layered slightly onto a plate. Place 1 egg on each tostada. Ladle generous amounts of warm salsa over the top.**
- **For *huevos divorciados* (divorced eggs), one side will be a red salsa and the other a green salsa. In the center, you can add beans or a thin beefsteak.**

# Chiles Seco

## DRIED CHILES

Welcome to the realm of dried chiles, the soul of Mexican salsas, where sun-kissed peppers transform into concentrated bursts of flavor. In this chapter, we'll explore the smoky depths of Salsa Macha (page 74), the fiery kick of Salsa Brava (page 71) and Mom's Toasted Chile de Arbol Salsa (page 72), and the unique nuttiness of Salsa de Cacahuate (page 85).

From the rich, dark Salsa Negra Martajada (page 79) to the fruity tang of Chamoy de Mango (page 86), these salsas showcase the incredible versatility of dried chiles. We'll also delve into dishes that highlight their power, like the comforting Chilaquiles Rojos (page 88), the devilishly spicy Camarónes à la Diabla (page 91), and the hearty Costillas de Res en Salsa (page 87), proving that dried chiles are the key to unlocking bold, unforgettable flavors.

# Salsa Brava

Does *chile piquin* intimidate you? That's understandable, but it doesn't have to put you off. There are still some chile peppers that I shy away from — Hatch green chiles, for instance — because of their heat levels. *Chile piquin* is spicy, but I have never found it so spicy that I couldn't enjoy it when it's blended with the right ingredients. This style of spicy salsa is for garnishing, and is great on tacos, but I wouldn't serve it with chips. And, remember, a little goes a long way!

PREP TIME: **25 MINUTES**
COOK TIME: **20 MINUTES**
YIELD: **1½ CUPS**

2 ounces dried *chile piquin*

1 pound (about 8 medium) tomatillos, husked

2 cloves garlic

½ teaspoon kosher or sea salt

In a small skillet over medium heat, toast the dried *chile piquin* for 3 to 4 minutes, stirring often. Set aside.

In another skillet over medium-high heat, add the tomatillos. Dry roast, turning as needed, for 20 minutes. Some blackening and blistering is encouraged. Set aside.

In the *molcajete*, add the garlic and salt. Grind them to a paste. Add the toasted *chile piquin* and continue grinding until you achieve a coarse-looking paste.

Coarsely chop the tomatillos. Gradually grind the tomatillos in the *molcajete* until you have a mostly smooth salsa. Using a wooden spoon, mix in a little water to thin out and loosen the salsa. Taste for salt.

TIPS & VARIATIONS

- **Keep the dried *chile piquin* in an airtight storage bag or container in a cool, dry place. Exposure to light will cause the peppers to fade and become brittle.**
- **If you can find fresh *chile piquin*, use it instead of the dried peppers in this recipe. Finely chop ½ cup white onion and 2 tablespoons of fresh cilantro. Mix them in after you process the salsa according to the instructions above.**

# Mom's Toasted Chile de Arbol Salsa

On special nights, Mom would prepare Dad a large pan-seared steak. This super-easy toasted *chile de arbol* salsa was a must-have on those nights. This was one of the rare times she used tomato sauce to prepare salsa. I imagine that she did this for convenience, but the results were delicious.

PREP TIME: **10 MINUTES**
COOK TIME: **15 MINUTES**
YIELD: **1½ CUPS**

10 dried *chile de arbol*

One 8-ounce can tomato sauce

1 clove garlic

1 tablespoon fresh lime juice (½ large lime)

Salt, to taste

Preheat the griddle to medium for 3 minutes. Remove the stems, if any, from the *chile de arbol* and place them on the hot griddle. Toss them often for 2 minutes; some blackening is desirable. If the griddle begins to smoke, reduce the heat. Do not let the chiles burn.

Transfer the chiles to a blender, add all the remaining ingredients, and blend until smooth. If the salsa is too thick, pour in a little water.

Transfer the mixture to a pot and cook over medium-low heat for 6 to 7 minutes.

Cool completely before storing in an airtight container for up to 9 days in the refrigerator.

Serve with your favorite beef tacos!

TIPS & VARIATIONS

- **Thin out this salsa recipe with 1 cup of chicken stock, and it can double as a spicy salsa for *chiles rellenos*, enchiladas, and *camarónes â la diabla*.**
- **Swap the tomato sauce for 3 Roma tomatoes poached in simmering water at medium heat for 10 minutes. When you are ready to blend, combine the tomatoes with the *chile de arbol*, 2 cloves of garlic, and 1 cup fatty beef stock from cooking *barbacoa*. Salt to taste. The beef stock is a taqueria secret for delicious red salsa on *barbacoa* tacos!**

# Salsa Taquera

This *chile de arbol* salsa is commonly found in many taquerias. You can make it with any dried or fresh chiles, and instead of citric acid powder, I sometimes use equal parts white vinegar and water. The citric acid or vinegar helps to preserve the salsa, extending its shelf life. The carrots add body to the mixture and just a hint of sweetness, which pairs well with the spicy *chile de arbol*.

PREP TIME: **20 MINUTES**
COOK TIME: **22 MINUTES**
YIELD: **2½ CUPS**

- 1 tablespoon avocado oil
- 1 small carrot, peeled and thinly sliced
- ¼ small onion, thinly sliced
- 5 cloves garlic, minced
- 1½ ounces *chile de arbol*, stemmed
- ½ teaspoon garlic powder
- ½ teaspoon onion powder
- ½ teaspoon pepper
- ¼ teaspoon oregano
- 1½ teaspoons salt, plus more to taste
- 1 teaspoon citric acid powder

In a skillet over medium heat, pour in the oil. After about 1 minute, add the carrots, onion, and garlic. Sauté, stirring as needed for the next 5 to 6 minutes, or until the ingredients begin to caramelize slightly.

Add the *chile de arbol* to one side of the skillet. Stir gently for 1 minute, then incorporate with the rest of the ingredients and continue cooking for 1 to 2 minutes.

Pour in 1½ cups of water. Stir to combine. Mix in the garlic powder, onion powder, pepper, oregano, and salt. Stir to combine. Bring the ingredients up to a light simmer, then remove from the heat and let stand for 10 minutes.

When ready, transfer everything, including the liquid, to a blender jar.

Pour in another ⅓ cup of water. Add another 1½ teaspoons of salt and 1 teaspoon of citric acid. Cover and blend on high until the mixture is very smooth.

Pour the salsa into a saucepan over medium heat. Bring to a light simmer and continue cooking for 10 minutes. Taste for salt. If you like a loose consistency, add a little more water.

Remove from the heat and let cool on the counter. Pour the salsa into lidded glass jars and store, refrigerated, for 6 to 8 months.

### TIPS & VARIATIONS

- **If you do not want to cook with citric acid, substitute ⅓ cup of distilled white vinegar for ⅓ cup of the water used in the cooking method.**
- **For a milder version of this dish, substitute half the *chile de arbol* with *chile cascabel* or chile California dried chile pods.**

# Salsa Macha

*Salsa macha* is essentially a salsa prepared by frying dried chiles and garlic, then blending them with oil. It is like an Asian chile oil that you see in supermarkets. The flavor will vary depending on what peppers you use and what other ingredients you add. It is a salsa made popular in Veracruz, Mexico, where cooks like to use the mostly all-smoky *chile morita* peppers. It's tasty with tacos, but I also use this *salsa macha* to mix into marinades, vinaigrettes, soups, and stews.

PREP TIME: **10 MINUTES**
COOK TIME: **20 MINUTES**
YIELD: **2½ CUPS**

2 cups avocado or extra-virgin olive oil

2 ounces dried *chile de arbol*, stemmed

2 ounces dried *chile morita*

6 cloves garlic

¼ cup apple cider vinegar

Salt, to taste

In a saucepan, combine the oil, *chile de arbol*, *chile morita*, and garlic over medium-low heat.

After a few minutes, when the peppers become aromatic, lower the heat slightly. Stir the peppers around every minute. Some of the peppers will become bright red and slightly soft. Do not let them get too dark, or they will taste bitter.

Season the vinegar with salt. Pour the mixture into the saucepan and stir to combine. Remove from the heat and let cool.

Once cool, transfer the mixture to a blender. Pulse to blend, adding more oil if the texture is too thick. Taste for salt.

TIPS & VARIATIONS

- **Salsa Macha will last up to 6 months stored in glass jars on the counter. It freezes almost indefinitely!**
- **For a milder version of this salsa, substitute half of the spicy *chile de arbol* with *chile guajillo*.**
- **Add more texture and flavor by mixing in 5 to 6 ounces unsalted roasted peanuts, pumpkin seeds, or sesame seeds to the *salsa macha* in the last 4 minutes of cooking time. You can combine all 3 or just add 1 of the ingredients. Blend as instructed.**
- **Whisk with Mexican *crema*, mayonnaise, and lime juice to serve alongside Mexican seafood dishes or mix a spoonful into a bowl of *menudo* or *pozole*. Delicious!**

# Smoky Chile Morita Salsa

I will never forget the first time I witnessed my *Tia* Minerva toasting a dried chipotle pod in a little oil. It changed my whole salsa-making life! The frying or toasting of any dried chile pod brings out its natural oils and yields a delicious, toasted-smoky flavor, taking your salsa and sauce recipes to the next level.

PREP TIME: **15 MINUTES**
COOK TIME: **28 MINUTES**
YIELD: **2 CUPS**

6 *chile morita*, stemmed

3 tablespoons avocado or olive oil

8 ounces (about 2 large) Roma tomatoes, halved

4 ounces (about 3 medium) tomatillos, halved

⅓ medium white onion, sliced

3 cloves garlic

2 tablespoons apple cider vinegar

Pinch of oregano

Salt, to taste

In a medium skillet, lightly fry the *chile morita* in the 1½ tablespoons of the oil over medium-low heat until soft. The chiles will look blistered and should inflate slightly, becoming aromatic and soft. Add the tomatoes, tomatillos, onion, and garlic. Sauté for 3 minutes, stirring often. Add 1¼ cups water.

Bring the mixture to a light boil and cook for 10 minutes before transferring to a blender. Add the vinegar, oregano, and salt. Blend on high until smooth.

Using the same skillet, heat the remaining 1½ tablespoons of oil over medium heat. Pour in the *salsa morita* from the blender and sear in the oil. Stir well to combine, and cook for 10 minutes. Season with salt.

Store refrigerated for up to 2 weeks in a lidded glass jar.

TIPS & VARIATIONS

- **At the end of the day, most cooked salsa recipes can be blended until they are very smooth or left a bit coarser. Adding 2 to 3 tablespoons of distilled white vinegar to any cooked salsa recipe will extend the life of the salsa for 3 to 4 weeks.**
- **Although *chile morita* and chipotle are similar in flavor, the *chile morita* can be a bit smokier and spicier.**

# Spicy New Mexico Salsa

In my years of cooking with dried chiles, I have come to learn their many differences. I truly love them all and choose certain varieties depending on what flavor profile I want to achieve. Dried chile New Mexico can range from medium to extra hot, so when I'm looking for an intense pepper flavor, I tend to reach for these pepper pods.

PREP TIME: **25 MINUTES**
COOK TIME: **25 MINUTES**
YIELD: **4 CUPS**

10 serrano peppers

½ medium white onion

6 cloves garlic

2 teaspoons avocado oil

18 ounces (about 16 medium) tomatillos

9 New Mexico chile pepper pods

Salt, to taste

Line a large griddle or skillet with aluminum foil and heat to medium. Add the peppers, onion, and garlic. Drizzle with 1 teaspoon of the oil and toss to coat evenly.

Add the washed tomatillos to a pot filled with 5 cups of water. Bring them up to a light boil at medium heat. Cook the tomatillos until they turn from bright green to an olive-green color. Cover and set aside for 10 minutes.

After 10 minutes, add the chile pepper pods to one side of the griddle with the other ingredients. Drizzle the remaining 1 teaspoon oil over the dried chiles. Continue roasting the chiles for 3 minutes, or until you see some blackening in spots. Flip often as they toast.

Transfer chile pods to the pot with tomatillos in hot water. Let soak for 5 minutes.

Transfer the red chile pods to the blender with 1 cup of the warm tomatillo water. Blend on high until smooth. Drain the tomatillos and transfer to the blender jar along with the remaining salsa ingredients.

Season with salt and blend on medium-high until mostly smooth.

Cook the blended salsa in a saucepan at medium heat for 10 minutes. Taste for salt. Let cool before storing in airtight glass jars, refrigerated for 14 to 16 days.

### TIPS & VARIATIONS

- **Make it a habit of storing salsa, sauces, and adobos in glass jars in the coldest part of the refrigerator. Plastic containers absorb odors and can become stained from the red chile peppers.**
- **To yield a milder version of this recipe, reduce the serrano peppers by half and substitute *guajillo* pepper pods for the chile New Mexico pods.**

# Salsa Negra Martajada

What is *salsa martajada*? *Salsa martajada* refers to a salsa that has been ground by hand using a volcanic-rock mortar and pestle, a *molcajete*. *Negra* means "black," referring to the chiles that almost look black in their dried state. Toasting the dried chiles will yield some blistering and blackening. Realistically, the finished *salsa negra* has different shades of brown, rust, red, and almost black tones. It's a beautiful salsa! Serve with your favorite grilled beef, pork, or chicken tacos.

PREP TIME: **35 MINUTES**
COOK TIME: **25 MINUTES**
YIELD: **2 CUPS**

2 long dried *chile negro*, seeded and stemmed

12 dried smoky *chile morita* (with seeds)

9 ounces (about 8 medium) tomatillos, husked

6 cloves garlic

1 teaspoon avocado oil

1 teaspoon coarse sea salt, plus more to taste

On a large griddle over medium heat, space all the dried chiles out evenly. After a few minutes, the chiles will become aromatic and start toasting. Turn as needed for the next 2 minutes, making sure they don't burn.

At the same time, bring 4 cups of water to a simmer over medium heat.

Transfer the chiles to the water. Let them soak while you finish preparing the other ingredients.

On the same hot griddle, add a section of aluminum foil. Place the tomatillos and garlic on the griddle. Drizzle the oil on them so they roast a little faster. Turn as needed for 20 minutes, removing the garlic after 15 minutes. Carefully wrap the foil around the tomatillos for 10 minutes. This will help them to cook through.

When cool, remove the outer husk from the garlic cloves and transfer them to the *molcajete*. Add the salt. Grind into a paste. Coarsely chop the tomatillos for easier grinding in the *molcajete*.

Gradually add a few of the softened chiles to the *molcajete* and grind them down as best you can. Then grind in the cooked tomatillos with the chiles and garlic. If the salsa is too thick, mix in a little bit of water until you have the desired consistency. Season with salt.

### TIPS & VARIATIONS

- **For a shortcut to this recipe, you can use chipotles in adobo that come in a can. I believe the *moritas* are smokier and carry more heat, but chipotles in adobo are still delicious!**
- **Mix in some finely chopped onion and chopped cilantro with cubed avocado for an over-the-top *molcajete salsa*! To achieve a smoother salsa, use a blender to mix.**

# Chile Puya Tomatillo Salsa

This salsa prepared with *chile puya* and tomatillos is currently my favorite salsa! It's a must for taco night! It has a nice bite, but it is not overly spicy. I like spicy food though, so it may be spicy for your taste. You can add fewer *chile puya* or mix in some *chile guajillo* to yield a milder salsa. A big thank you to my friend Patty for sharing this delicious salsa combination with me! I prepare it at least once every ten days. It's that good!

PREP TIME: **10 MINUTES**
COOK TIME: **15 MINUTES**
YIELD: **2 CUPS**

1 pound (about 11 medium) tomatillos, husked and washed

1 tablespoon avocado oil

12 *chile puya*, stemmed

4 cloves garlic

Small bunch of fresh cilantro

Salt, to taste

Transfer the tomatillos into a medium saucepan with 4 cups of simmering water. Cook for 10 minutes, or until the tomatillos turn from bright green to an olive-green color. Remove from the heat.

In a separate skillet, heat the oil to medium heat. Remove the stems from the *chile puya* and transfer to the skillet. Toss the chiles often so they don't burn. They should be aromatic and change slightly in color. Some chiles will become bright red, others may appear darker. Use tongs to transfer them to the blender jar. In that same oil, add the garlic and sauté for 3 to 4 minutes. Transfer the garlic to the blender with the chiles.

Pour 1 cup of the warm cooking water from the reserved tomatillo into the blender. Blend on high until it is very smooth. You may need to scrape down the sides or add a little more water so it blends smoothly. Drain all the water from the remaining tomatillos and transfer them to the blender. Add cilantro and salt to taste. Again, blend on high until it is very smooth. Taste for salt. Pour into a serving bowl.

Transfer the blended salsa to a pot and heat to medium. When it comes up to a boil, reduce the heat and continue cooking the salsa for 8 to 10 minutes. Cool completely and then pour the salsa into airtight glass jars. Store in the refrigerator for up to 14 days.

TIPS & VARIATIONS

- **Toast dried peppers quickly by drizzling a little bit of avocado oil into a preheated skillet. Toss vigorously for 10 seconds. Remove immediately. Burnt peppers can be bitter tasting.**

# Chile Cascabel Salsa

The *cascabel* chile-pepper pod is round. And when you shake it, the sound resembles a rattlesnake shaking its tail. The chile is generally mild, and it yields a nutty flavor when toasted. This pepper is not as readily available as some other dried-pepper varieties, but there are good sources online where you can purchase the *cascabel*.

PREP TIME: **15 MINUTES**
COOK TIME: **40 MINUTES**
YIELD: **2 CUPS**

4 ounces *cascabel* peppers, seeded and stemmed

8 *chile de arbol* peppers, seeded and stemmed

14 ounces (about 6) tomatillos, husked

3 cloves garlic, skin on

Salt, to taste

3 tablespoons avocado or extra-virgin olive oil

½ cup finely chopped white onion

In a medium saucepan, heat 4 cups of water over medium heat.

On a preheated griddle or skillet over medium heat, dry roast both dried chile varieties, the tomatillos, and the garlic. Toast the peppers just until they become aromatic and change color slightly. This takes just a few minutes. Press the peppers with a metal spatula to help them roast a little faster.

As soon as the peppers are aromatic, transfer them to the pot of simmering water. Simmer for 10 minutes and then let them stand in the water while you roast the tomatillos. Continue roasting the tomatillos and garlic for 15 minutes. Turn as needed. Let cool, then remove the skin from the garlic. Set aside.

Using a slotted spoon, transfer the *chile cascabel* and *chile de arbol* to a blender. Add 1 cup of the cooking water used to soften the peppers. Blend on high until the mixture is very smooth.

To the blender jar, add the garlic, tomatillos, and salt. Blend on high until smooth.

Preheat the oil over medium heat. After a few minutes, pour in the salsa from the blender. Reduce the heat to a slow simmer and cook for 7 to 10 minutes. Transfer to a serving bowl and top with chopped onion.

TIPS & VARIATIONS

- **The milder *chile cascabel* by itself is best in adobos, for braising meats, or in soups. Mixed with spicier peppers like *chile de arbol* or *piquin* yields a delicious salsa.**
- **Toast and then grind 8 ounces of *chile cascabel* that have had the stemmed. An inexpensive coffee grinder works great for preparing this pure chile powder. Substitute this fresh ground powder in any recipe that calls for chili powder.**

# Salsa Campechana

*Salsa campechana* is an easy translation: *campechana* describes something that is made up of different components or ingredients. The result of this *salsa campechana* gives the appearance of a salsa ground in a *molcajete*, a lava-rock mortar and pestle. Instead, with a few quick pulses from your food processor, this salsa made of authentic and fresh ingredients is ready!

PREP TIME: **20 MINUTES**
COOK TIME: **23 MINUTES**
YIELD: **4 CUPS**

1½ pounds (about 16 medium) tomatillos, husked

⅓ large white onion, sliced into thick rings

6 cloves garlic

2 *guajillo* peppers, seeded and stemmed

1 cup *chile de arbol*, stemmed

Handful of fresh cilantro

Salt, to taste

In a medium saucepan, heat 4 cups of water over medium-low heat.

On a griddle or large skillet over medium heat, add the tomatillos, onion, garlic, *chile guajillo*, and *chile de arbol*. Dry roast everything for 20 minutes, removing the *guajillos* and *arbol* after 1 to 2 minutes. Remove onion and garlic after 10 minutes. Continue cooking the tomatillos for another 10 minutes. Turn as needed.

Transfer the dried chiles to the saucepan of simmering water and cook for 7 minutes.

When ready, transfer the chiles and 1 cup of the cooking water to a food processor or blender. Blend them for 1 minute. Add the tomatillos, onion, and garlic. Pulse to achieve a chunky salsa.

Add the cilantro to the blender jar and salt to taste. Pulse to achieve a *molcajete*-style-looking salsa. If you prefer your salsa smoother, then blend on high. If the consistency is too thick, pour in a little more water.

### TIPS & VARIATIONS

- **A food processor and blender will produce different results. Using a food processor will create a salsa that looks as if it's been prepared in a *molcajete*. The pulse button on a blender will give you a coarse-looking salsa, but still a bit smoother.**
- **The more you toast and blacken the ingredients, the darker the appearance of the salsa will be. For a brighter red look, gently boil the ingredients until soft and then follow the instructions for blending.**

# Salsa de Cacahuate

*Salsa de cacahuate*, aka peanut salsa! Not all of us associate peanuts with a spicy salsa, but in Mexican cuisine it is common to combine nuts and seeds with dried chiles. Delicious recipes, such as traditional mole and red *pipián*, are just two recipes that combine nuts and dried chile pods. When writing this recipe, I realized it had been a while since I had prepared a salsa de *cacahuate*. I had almost forgotten how much I enjoy it! Serve over your favorite tacos, burritos, or tostadas.

PREP TIME: **35 MINUTES**
COOK TIME: **30 MINUTES**
YIELD: **2 CUPS**

4 ounces (¾ cup) unsalted peanuts

3 to 4 tablespoons extra-virgin olive oil

¼ medium onion

4 cloves garlic

1 teaspoon peppercorns

¾ ounces *chile de arbol*

1½ ounces *chile cascabel*, seeded, stemmed, and torn into small pieces

¼ cup apple cider vinegar

Pinch of oregano

Salt, to taste

Shell the peanuts, making sure to also remove the peanut husks.

Add 1 tablespoon of the oil to a skillet and preheat to medium for 1 to 2 minutes. When ready, add the onion, garlic, and peppercorns. Sauté for 3 to 5 minutes. Transfer to a blender jar.

In that same skillet, pour in 1 more tablespoon of oil. Add the peanuts. Continue cooking at medium heat for 5 minutes, stirring often. Transfer the peanuts to the blender jar.

Again, in the same skillet, pour in 1 more tablespoon of oil. Add the *chile de arbol* and *chile cascabel*. Fry and toast, stirring often for 3 to 4 minutes. Add 1 cup of water. When the mixture comes to a simmer, cover the pan with a lid and remove it from the heat. Let the chiles soak for 10 minutes.

When ready, transfer the chiles with all the liquid to the blender jar. Pour in the vinegar, 1 more cup of water, and oregano. Blend on high until very smooth. Season with salt. If the salsa is too thick, mix in a little more water. Store salsa in a glass mason jar refrigerated for up to 10 days.

### TIPS & VARIATIONS

- **To yield a milder salsa, reduce the *chile de arbol* to ¼ ounce (14 peppers) and add ½ ounce (2 peppers) *chile guajillo*.**
- **This is not only a tasty garnish for your favorite tacos, but also a delicious spicy peanut sauce for braising chicken thighs. Dilute the salsa with 2 cups of chicken stock. Sear and brown 3 pounds Transfer to a baking dish. Pour in the diluted salsa. Cover and braise in a 350°F oven for 45 minutes.**

# Chamoy de Mango

*Chamoy* is a type of salsa prepared with dried hibiscus, fresh or dried fruits, dried chile-pepper pods, and spices. Most often you will see it drizzled over fresh-fruit and vegetable cups filled with mango, pineapple, cucumber, jicama, and watermelon. It makes a delicious garnish for the rim on Mexican-style cocktails.

PREP TIME: **25 MINUTES**
COOK TIME: **25 MINUTES**
YIELD: **4½ CUPS**

1 cup dried hibiscus

1 large mango, peeled and cubed (about 10 ounces)

⅓ cup craisins

1 large dried *ancho* pepper, seeded and stemmed

12 dried *arbol* peppers, stemmed

⅓ cup chile-lime seasoning powder

2 tablespoons fresh lime juice (1 large lime)

Salt, to taste

Transfer the dried hibiscus to a saucepan. Cover with 3 cups of water. Bring to a boil over medium heat. Reduce the heat and simmer for 5 minutes. Remove from the heat.

In another saucepan, add the cubed mango, craisins, and dried chiles. Cover with 4 cups of water. Bring to a boil over medium heat. Reduce to a simmer and cook for 10 minutes.

When ready, drain and reserve the liquid from the dried hibiscus. Give the hibiscus a quick rinse under cool water. Reserve the softened hibiscus.

Remove all the mango and chiles from the pot. Reserve 1 cup of the cooking water.

When ready, to the blender add the softened hibiscus, mango, craisins, peppers, chile-lime seasoning, lime juice, 2 cups of the reserved hibiscus water, and 1 cup of the mango cooking water. Blend on high until the texture is very smooth.

Transfer to a saucepan and cook at medium heat for 10 minutes. Taste for salt. Once cooled, transfer the salsa to glass jars. It will keep in the refrigerator for up to 8 months.

### TIPS & VARIATIONS

- **Prepare different fruit flavors by substituting pineapple, strawberries, apricots, or peaches for the mango. You can use fresh or unsweetened dried fruits.**
- **The *chamoy* sauce can be stored in the freezer for up to 1 year in an airtight container.**
- **Change the heat level by adding more *arbol* chile peppers or omitting them altogether.**
- **For a vegetarian version, substitute the beef with sliced portabella mushrooms, roasted poblano peppers, and sliced zucchini.**
- **For stewed recipes, jarred *nopales* (cactus) work well if fresh are unavailable.**
- **Pork country-style ribs are also delicious here.**

# Costillas de Res en Salsa

## BEEF RIBS WITH CACTUS IN SALSA

*Costillas con nopalitos* translates to ribs with cactus. It is very popular to use pork ribs, but on this occasion, I am using beef flanken short ribs. They are thin-sliced beef short ribs that make this recipe delicious. There is something so enticing about fall-off-the-bone-tender rib meat simmered in salsa. The texture and flavor of the cactus are an excellent addition to any stewed meat dish. Serve with rice, beans, and flour tortillas.

PREP TIME: **30 MINUTES**
COOK TIME: **1 HOUR**
YIELD: **6 SERVINGS**

3 tablespoons avocado oil

1 medium white onion, sliced

4 cloves garlic, peeled and minced

5 *chile negro*, seeded and stemmed

2 *chile ancho*, seeded and stemmed

10 ounces (about 5) tomatillos, husked, washed, and sliced into quarters

2 pounds beef flanken short ribs, sliced into pieces

Salt and pepper, to taste

2 teaspoons chicken bouillon

Pinch of oregano

3 cups cooked *nopalitos* (cactus paddles), sliced into strips (see Nopalitos en Salsa recipe, page 59)

In a pot over medium heat, add 1 tablespoon of the oil. Add ¼ of the sliced onion and half of the minced garlic. Sauté for 3 minutes. Add the *chile negro*, *chile ancho*, and tomatillos. Sauté for another 3 minutes. Pour in 3 cups of water. Bring up to a simmer and cook for 8 minutes. Remove from the heat and let sit for 10 minutes.

In a large sauté pan, heat the remaining 2 tablespoons of oil to medium heat.

Season the beef ribs lightly with salt and pepper. Sear and brown the ribs, turning as needed.

Transfer all but 1 cup of the cooking water to the ingredients from the skillet into the blender jar. Season with the bouillon, oregano, and salt and pepper to taste. Blend on high until it is very smooth. Taste for salt. Set aside.

Add the reserved sliced onion to the beef. Sauté for 2 to 3 minutes. Add the reserved garlic and sauté for 1 more minute.

Add cactus and the salsa from the blender. Stir well to combine. Reduce the heat to a light simmer. Cover partially and continue cooking for 35 to 40 minutes or until the beef is tender.

# Chilaquiles Rojos

*Chilaquiles*! I absolutely love them! They are yet another tortilla- or corn-*masa*-based recipe that is inexpensive to prepare. You can go simple with the *chilaquiles* by garnishing with Mexican *crema* and crumbled *queso fresco* or add your favorite protein, such as *bistec*! Either way, make sure you prepare your own thick *totopos* (tortilla chips) or find a thick, good-quality store-bought chip.

PREP TIME: **25 MINUTES**
COOK TIME: **33 MINUTES**
YIELD: **2 SERVINGS**

1 cup avocado or vegetable oil

6 corn tortillas

1¼ cups Salsa Roja (page 94)

2 large eggs

Salt, to taste

⅛ teaspoon pepper

2 tablespoons finely diced onion

⅓ cup *queso fresco*, crumbled

⅓ cup Mexican *crema*

1 tablespoon finely chopped cilantro

1 medium avocado, sliced

Preheat the oil in a medium skillet over medium heat for 5 to 6 minutes. Slice the corn tortillas into wedges and fry them for 7 minutes, turning as needed. Transfer to a plate lined with paper towels. Set the fried chips aside. Reserve the oil.

In a saucepan, preheat 2 tablespoons of reserved oil over medium heat for a few minutes.

Once the oil is hot, pour in the salsa. Stir well to combine. Reduce the heat to low to keep warm.

In a separate skillet over medium heat, preheat 2 tablespoons of reserved oil for 3 minutes. Crack the eggs into the skillet. Season lightly with salt and the pepper. Cover the skillet with a lid and cook the eggs to desired doneness.

Add the fried chips to the warm salsa. Stir well to combine until all the chips are evenly coated. Reduce the heat slightly and cook for 3 minutes.

Divide the *chilaquiles* onto two plates. Top each with a fried egg, onion, *queso fresco*, *crema*, cilantro, avocado, and a pinch of salt. Enjoy!

### TIPS & VARIATIONS

- **Slice the corn tortillas one day in advance and dry them on the counter. The dried tortillas will fry up faster and absorb less oil when fried.**
- **Any cooked salsas or sauce recipes that are smooth are delicious in *chilaquiles*.**

TIPS & VARIATIONS

- For a milder version of this recipe, reduce the quantity of *chile de arbol* to 2 or 3. Add 2 large, roasted Roma tomatoes. Season with salt and pepper.
- To roast the poblano pepper, drizzle it with a little avocado oil. Place it on a lined baking sheet. Place under the broiler for 9 to 10 minutes, turning as needed.
- Toss some cooked linguini in ⅓ cup pasta water and add the cooked shrimp. Cook for 1 minute. Top with the grated cheese of your choice.

# Camarónes à la Diabla

*Camarónes á la diabla*, or "deviled shrimp." I developed this recipe a few years back, originally serving it with rice and corn tortillas. It later became a filling for flaky, baked empanadas. Since then, the recipe has varied from time to time, depending on which ingredients I have on hand.

Many traditional recipes for *camarónes á la diabla* include roasted or poached tomatoes in the blended sauce. I decided that if it's called *diablo* shrimp, then it should be a pure chile sauce with no tomatoes. You can certainly add roasted tomatoes though, if you like. Serve over rice.

PREP TIME: **35 MINUTES**
COOK TIME: **1 HOUR**
YIELD: **6 SERVINGS**

2½ pounds shrimp, peeled and cleaned

Salt and pepper, to taste

3 tablespoons avocado or extra-virgin olive oil

1 small white onion, coarsely chopped

6 cloves garlic, coarsely chopped

6 chile California, seeded, stemmed, and coarsely torn

6 *chile de arbol*, stemmed

3 cups seafood or chicken stock

½ teaspoon ground cumin

¾ teaspoon Mexican oregano

1 large poblano pepper, roasted, peeled, and thinly sliced (optional)

Small handful of fresh cilantro, minced

Rinse the shrimp under cold water, patting them dry with paper towels. Season with salt and pepper. Keep chilled until ready to use.

In a large skillet, preheat the oil over medium heat for 2 minutes. Add the onion and cook for 3 minutes. Add the garlic, chile California, and *chile de arbol*. Sauté for 1 to 2 minutes, stirring constantly. Pour in 1½ cups of the stock. Bring to a simmer for 10 minutes. Remove from the heat and let stand for 10 minutes.

Transfer all the ingredients from the skillet to a blender. Pour in another 1½ cups of the stock. Add the cumin and oregano. Blend on high until smooth.

Return the blended salsa to the skillet. Heat over medium-low heat, and after it comes to a simmer, season with salt and pepper. Continue cooking for 25 minutes, until the mixture reduces and thickens.

Fold in the chilled shrimp. Cook at a simmer, stirring as needed, for 5 to 6 minutes. Once the shrimp turns pink and opaque, fold in the roasted poblano pepper (if using). Cook 1 minute more, then garnish with cilantro.

# Sauces & Adobos

Welcome to a culinary journey through the heart of Mexican flavor, where salsas and adobos paint the palate with vibrant hues and bold spices. In this chapter, we'll explore the foundational flavors of classic Salsa Roja (page 94) and Salsa Verde (page 96), delve into the smoky depths of Salsa Chipotle (page 97) and Chile Ancho Salsa (page 99), and uncover the rich complexity of mole.

But we won't stop there. We'll discover the transformative power of adobos, from the savory chorizo adobo and Al Pastor Adobo (page 101) to the earthy Cochinita Pibil Adobo (page 108) and the vibrant Adobo Verde (page 107), all leading to dishes like the comforting Beef Birria (page 112), the hearty Enchiladas Rojas (page 118), and the festive Chile Colorado Pork Tamales (page 115). Get ready to infuse your kitchen with the soul of Mexico!

# Salsa Roja

Most of us imagine salsa as served with chips or as a garnish for tacos and the like. A sauce is most often incorporated into a dish, and it will be served warm or used for *guisados* (stews) or as a soup base. In Mexico, whether it's a salsa for chips and tacos, or if it's a sauce for enchiladas, they are both referred to as salsas.

PREP TIME: **25 MINUTES**
COOK TIME: **30 MINUTES**
YIELD: **5½ CUPS**

6 tablespoons avocado oil

½ medium white onion, coarsely sliced

4 cloves garlic, smashed

1¼ teaspoons cumin seeds

1¼ teaspoons oregano

1¼ teaspoons ground peppercorns

10 California chile or *guajillo* chile pods, seeded and stemmed

2 *ancho* chile pods, seeded and stemmed

6 *arbol* chile pods, stemmed

Salt, to taste

Preheat 3 tablespoons of the oil in a deep skillet over medium heat. After 1 to 2 minutes, add the onion and garlic. Sauté for 3 to 4 minutes. Add the cumin, oregano, and peppercorns. Sauté for 1 minute more. Incorporate all the chile pods and sauté, moving vigorously for 2 minutes. Pour in 4 cups of water. Let everything come to a simmer, then cover the skillet and remove it from the heat. Let stand for 10 to 15 minutes, covered.

When ready, transfer all the ingredients from the skillet to a blender jar. Season with salt. Cover, then blend on high until smooth. I have a power blender, so there is no need to strain the sauce. If you don't, blend for an extra 2 minutes or strain the sauce through a fine-mesh sieve. Set aside.

In the same skillet, add the remaining 3 tablespoons of oil and preheat to medium for 2 minutes. Pour in the sauce from the blender jar. Stir well to combine, then bring to a simmer. Taste for salt and adjust to your liking. Reduce heat slightly and continue cooking for 10 minutes. Cool completely before storing in glass jars refrigerated for up to 2 weeks.

### TIPS & VARIATIONS

- **There are several variations when it comes to how the ingredients are cooked. Some are fried in oil, others softened in water or stock. This type of *salsa roja* recipe can be used for enchiladas, *chilaquiles*, *pozole*, *menudo*, or tamales or as a base for *caldos* (soups) of all kinds. There really is no exact recipe — that is the beauty of cooking.**
- **Add 2 large Roma tomatoes that have been roasted or poached to this recipe to bring a rich tomato flavor.**
- **Up the flavor further by including 1 teaspoon each of granulated garlic and granulated onion before blending.**

# Salsa Verde

Twice a year, when I was a child, my family and I traveled through Arizona and New Mexico on our cross-country trips from California to Monterrey, Mexico. This *salsa verde* is a combination of my love for Mexico and my love for the American Southwest. Great for enchiladas, pozole, pork *chile verde*, stews, soups, tamales, and any recipe that calls for a green chile sauce or *salsa verde*.

PREP TIME: **25 MINUTES**
COOK TIME: **50 MINUTES**
YIELD: **5 CUPS**

- 10 Anaheim peppers, seeded and stemmed
- 3 large poblano peppers, seeded and stemmed
- 5 tablespoons avocado oil
- 10 ounces (about 5) tomatillos
- 1 medium white onion, coarsely chopped
- 6 cloves garlic
- 6 serrano chile peppers, seeded and stemmed
- 2 teaspoons crushed cumin seeds
- 3 cups chicken or vegetable stock
- ⅓ cup *masa harina*
- Salt, to taste

Preheat the broiler on high.

Lay the Anaheim and poblano peppers on a baking sheet lined with aluminum foil. Drizzle with 2 teaspoons of the oil. Transfer the baking sheet onto the top rack under the broiler. Broil for 10 minutes or until most of the skins have blistered, flipping over halfway through the cooking time. Remove the peppers from the oven and cover with a clean kitchen towel to sweat and cool for 10 minutes.

In a medium pot, combine the tomatillos, onion, garlic, and serrano peppers. Cover with 4 cups of water. Bring to a boil over medium heat. Reduce the heat to low and continue cooking until the tomatillos change color. Remove them from the heat.

Peel the blistered skins from the peppers and give them a rough chop. Drain the tomatillos. In the blender jar, add the peppers, tomatillos, onion, garlic, serranos, cumin seeds, broth, masa harina, and salt. Blend on high until smooth.

In a large saucepan over medium heat, preheat the remaining 3 tablespoons of oil. Pour the *salsa verde* into the hot oil. Stir well to combine. Bring up to a light boil, then reduce the heat to low. Continue cooking sauce, stirring as needed, for an additional 20 minutes. The sauce will become thicker.

## TIPS & VARIATIONS

- **For a charred-looking *chile verde* sauce, roast or grill all the fresh ingredients. Remove the seeds and stems from the peppers, but do not remove the blistered skin. Using a power blender, like a Vitamix, blend, strain, and cook as instructed.**

# Salsa Chipotle

Chipotle peppers have a distinct smoky flavor that pairs well with both tomatoes and tomatillos in salsas and sauces. The flavor combinations in this chipotle sauce/salsa are popular in chicken *tinga*. But don't limit yourself to just that one dish, of course.

PREP TIME: **25 MINUTES**
COOK TIME: **50 MINUTES**
YIELD: **5½ CUPS**

- 5 to 6 tablespoons avocado oil or naturally rendered pork lard
- 3½ cups chicken stock
- 3 *chile guajillo* or chile California pods, seeded and stemmed
- ½ medium white onion, thinly sliced
- 5 cloves garlic, minced
- 20 ounces (about 5) Roma tomatoes, sliced into wedges
- Salt and pepper, to taste
- One 7-ounce can chipotles in adobo

In a large, deep skillet, add 2 tablespoons of the oil. Heat to medium. In a separate pot, heat the chicken stock over low heat.

Place the dried chile *guajillo* in the skillet. After a few minutes, they will begin to sizzle and become aromatic. Turn as needed for 1 to 2 minutes; they may blacken slightly.

Add the onions and garlic. Sauté for 3 minutes. Add the Roma tomatoes. Season with salt and pepper. Sauté for 5 more minutes, or until the tomatoes start to break down and release their juices. Pour in the warm stock. Remove from the heat and let the ingredients stand for 10 minutes.

Preheat the remaining 3 to 4 tablespoons of oil in a skillet over medium heat while you blend the sauce. Carefully pour the guajillos, onion, garlic, tomatoes, and all of the broth from the skillet into a blender jar and season with salt and pepper. Blend on high until very smooth. Pour into the skillet with the preheated oil. Stir well, then bring to a boil. Reduce the heat to below medium. Cover partially and continue cooking for 20 minutes, stirring occasionally. Taste for seasoning.

Cool the salsa completely before storing it in refrigerated glass jars for up to 10 days.

### TIPS & VARIATIONS

- **The *guajillos* are optional — I enjoy the bright-red color and flavor they bring.**
- **This sauce is perfect for low-and-slow braising of shredded chicken, and sliced beef or pork. The flavor profile of this chipotle salsa is traditional for a dish called *tinga de pollo*.**
- **For a milder version of the sauce, omit half the chipotles in adobo.**
- **Why do I fry the salsa in oil after blending? Flavor! Frying concentrates the flavors and cooks out any leftover impurities. For example, fried onion has more flavor than boiled onion. If you have never enjoyed a table salsa fried in naturally rendered pork lard, you don't know what you are missing! Cooking with naturally rendered pork lard is traditional and authentic in a Mexican kitchen.**

TIPS & VARIATIONS

- You can prepare any red chile salsa several months in advance of when you may be using it and store it in the freezer. The flavors will intensify and become even more delicious!
- As with any red chile salsa, combine different dried chile pods to create different flavor profiles: for instance, swap out 4 of the *chile ancho* for 5 chile California; to amp up the heat, add 10 *arbol chile* to the mix.
- This *chile ancho* salsa adds traditional, authentic flavors that have been used for generations to prepare pork tamales in Northern Mexico, where my parents were from.

# Chile Ancho Salsa

There must be a hundred recipes, if not more, explaining how to prepare a red chile sauce. My go-to is this *chile ancho* sauce. Mom favored *chile ancho* for some of the most traditional family dishes, so I'm very familiar with this chile. It is mostly mild, but with deep flavors. The distinct flavor of the salsa was in Mom's tamales, *chile colorado*, *menudo*, and *costillas de puerco* (pork ribs).

PREP TIME: **25 MINUTES**
COOK TIME: **53 MINUTES**
YIELD: **7 CUPS**

9 ounces (15 to 20) *ancho* chile pods, seeded and stemmed

5 cups chicken stock or water

½ tablespoon Mexican oregano

½ tablespoon cumin

6 cloves garlic

1½ teaspoons black pepper

Salt, to taste

¼ cup naturally rendered pork lard or avocado oil

Fill a large pot with 2 quarts of water. Bring it to a simmer over medium heat.

Place the *ancho* chile pods on a large, preheated griddle or skillet over medium heat. Flip them continuously for 1 to 2 minutes, then transfer them to the pot of simmering water. When the water begins to boil, reduce the heat to medium-low and cook for 8 minutes. The peppers will change slightly in color as they soften. Remove from the heat and let cool for 10 minutes before draining the water.

Place the peppers in a blender jar. Add the chicken stock, oregano, cumin, garlic, pepper, and salt to taste. Blend on high until smooth. Using a fine-mesh sieve, strain the sauce into a larger bowl, pressing all the pulp through with a wooden spoon. If you are using a power blender, there is no need to strain the salsa.

In a large pot, preheat the lard or oil over medium heat for a few minutes. Pour in the salsa from the blender. Bring to a boil, reduce the heat, and cook for 20 to 25 minutes.

Adjust the seasoning as the salsa cooks and becomes thicker. Cook for another 10 minutes.

Cool completely before storing in glass jars in the refrigerator for up to 14 days.

# Chorizo Norteño

You know how you have special food memories stuck in your head? They play over and over in your mind, so much so that you can see past images clearly, hear bygone sounds, even smell the aromas of the food? For me, the spicy, rustic *chorizo Norteño* that my *abuela* used to prepare does that. It's an absolute (and sentimental) favorite!

**PREP TIME: 1 HOUR, 30 MINUTES**
**COOK TIME: 15 MINUTES**
**DRYING TIME: 5 TO 6 DAYS**
**YIELD: 5 POUNDS CHORIZO**

9 ounces (15 to 20) dried *ancho* chile peppers, seeded and stemmed

5 pounds ground pork butt or shoulder

½ cup apple cider vinegar

½ cup distilled white vinegar

2 tablespoons Mexican oregano

2 tablespoons cumin seeds

2 tablespoons peppercorns

2 tablespoons crushed red pepper flakes

15 whole cloves

20 cloves garlic

3 tablespoons kosher salt, plus more to taste

In a large pot, simmer the chiles in 1½ quarts of water for 10 minutes, then remove from heat and let stand for 10 minutes.

Transfer the ground pork to a large ceramic bowl. In a large glass bowl, mix the apple cider and white vinegars; pour half over the pork, reserving the rest. Let stand for 35 minutes.

In a skillet over medium-low heat, combine the oregano, cumin seeds, peppercorns, red pepper flakes, and cloves. Stir for 3 minutes once aromatic, then remove from the heat.

Drain the *ancho* chiles and transfer them to a blender. Add all toasted spices, garlic, and reserved vinegar. Add 3 tablespoons of the salt, remembering the mixture needs to be salty to season the chorizo thoroughly. Pour in just enough water for a smooth adobo consistency; blend on high. Season with salt to taste.

Thoroughly mix 5 cups of adobo into the pork, wearing plastic gloves for best results. Test ¼ cup of chorizo by cooking in a skillet over medium heat for 7 to 8 minutes; season with salt to taste. Once the desired flavor is achieved, cook the remaining pork.

To make *Norteño*-style links, use a piping bag with a metal tip to fill 32-mm collagen casings. Pierce several holes with a toothpick to release excess liquid during drying. Hang for 5 to 6 days in a cool, dry space until links shrink.

For easy storage, freeze 8 to 9 ounces of the chorizo filling individually in flat, quart-size freezer bags for up to 5 months. Freezing intensifies the flavors, which will improve after 1 month.

TIPS & VARIATIONS

- **Drying chorizo intensifies the flavors of the spices. The texture of this chorizo is a little chunky, which is the desired texture for rustic recipes.**

# Al Pastor Adobo

In addition to *carne asada*, tacos *al pastor* is one of the most popular dishes in Mexico and the United States. The distinct bright-red adobo can be as simple as a few ingredients or it can be more complex, featuring different levels of flavors. It is really delicious when paired with pork.

PREP TIME: **20 MINUTES**
COOK TIME: **15 MINUTES**
YIELD: **3 CUPS**

½ medium white onion, sliced

4 cloves garlic, smashed

1 teaspoon avocado oil

5 dried *guajillo* chile peppers, seeded, stemmed, and coarsely torn

1 dried *ancho* chile peppers, seeded, stemmed, and coarsely torn

¼ cup *achiote* paste

4 chipotles in adobo

2 tablespoons adobo from chipotles

¼ cup apple cider or distilled white vinegar

Salt and pepper, to taste

Add the onion, garlic, and oil to a medium skillet over medium heat. Sauté for a few minutes, then add the torn chiles. Cook for 3 minutes, stirring. Pour in 2 cups of water. Cook for 6 to 7 minutes. Remove from the heat and let everything soak for 10 minutes.

Transfer all the ingredients to a blender. Add the *achiote* paste, chipotles in adobo, vinegar, and salt and pepper, to taste. Blend on high until smooth. If the adobo is too thick, mix in some more water. Taste for salt. It should be on the salty side to season the meat.

Pour the adobo into glass jars and refrigerate for a few weeks or freeze for a few months.

TIPS & VARIATIONS

- **Traditionally, thin slices of pork are marinated in adobo and then stacked on a rotisserie and spit-roasted. The charred meat is sliced from the outer edges and garnished with fresh or grilled pineapple and the spicy salsa.**
- **The adobo is not limited to pork. A little goes a long way as a marinade for chicken, shrimp, and fish.**

# Mole

I am confessing to you all right now: Mom didn't prepare mole from scratch! She, like millions of Mexican cooks, took a shortcut and purchased mole paste in a jar. Don't get me wrong, it's delicious and saves a lot of time, but I am a curious cook and a die-hard foodie, so I challenged myself years ago to learn how to prepare a basic mole recipe. This one includes many traditional ingredients, but know that every region, every family in Mexico will prepare their own unique recipe.

PREP TIME: **30 MINUTES**
COOK TIME: **3 HOURS, 30 MINUTES**
YIELD: **10 SERVINGS**

8 *ancho* or *mulato* chile pods

6 *negro* chile pods

6 *morita* chile pods

8 *puya* chile pods

1½ cups naturally rendered pork lard or avocado oil

½ *bolillo* bread roll, cubed

½ large white onion, coarsely chopped

6 cloves garlic

2 serrano peppers, stemmed

9 ounces (about 4) tomatillos, husked

7 ounces (about 2) Roma tomatoes

¼ cup *pepitas* (pumpkin seeds), shelled

¼ cup blanched almonds

¼ cup unsalted peanuts

½ cup sesame seeds, toasted

¼ cup raisins or dried plums

1½ teaspoons oregano

1½ teaspoons cumin seeds

½ teaspoon anise seeds

1-inch piece Mexican cinnamon stick

1½ teaspoons peppercorns

Salt, to taste

1½ ounces Mexican chocolate, coarsely chopped

Remove the stems and seeds from the large chile pods and only the stems from the small chile pods, then add them to a large, heavy pot. Drizzle in ¼ cup of the pork lard. Heat over medium heat for 1 to 2 minutes, or until the chiles begin to sizzle and become aromatic. Flip several times, gently pressing them to the bottom of the pot to toast and blister slightly. Transfer to another pot. Discard any seeds left in the pot.

Add another ¼ cup of the lard into the same pot. Drop in the cubed bread. Toss for a few minutes until toasted. Reserve it in the pot with the chiles.

To the pot, add the onion, garlic, serrano peppers, and tomatillo. Dry roast them for a few minutes before adding the tomatoes and a drizzle of lard. Let the ingredients char slightly, turning often.

continues on page 104

continued from page 102

Add the *pepitas*, almonds, peanuts, and sesame seeds to the pot. Add in a little more lard. Sauté and toast the nuts and seeds with the other ingredients for a few minutes.

Add the raisins, oregano, cumin seeds, anise seeds, cinnamon, and peppercorns. Fry for 3 to 4 minutes.

Pour 8 cups of water into the pot, gently stirring the ingredients. Add the reserved chiles and bread. Stir well; cook for 10 minutes. Remove the pot from the heat and let the mixture stand for 20 minutes.

In two batches, transfer the mixture from the pot into a blender jar. Blend on high until very smooth. If you are not using a power blender, you may have to blend longer. If the sauce is not smooth and creamy-looking, strain it through a fine-mesh sieve. Pour the batches of sauce into a large bowl. Add 2 cups of water to the blender jar and swish it around to catch any sauce left in the jar, then add it to the bowl. Stir to combine. Set aside.

Wipe out the large pot. Add the remaining ⅓ cup of pork lard and preheat over medium heat. Once the lard is hot, pour in the reserved sauce. Take care, as it will splatter. Stir well to combine. Season with salt, adding a little at a time, letting the mole cook for a few minutes before seasoning again.

Add the chocolate. Once it has melted, taste for seasoning. Reduce the heat to simmer for the next 3 hours, or until the mole reduces and becomes the rich, dark color you want.

Let the sauce cool before storing it in an airtight container. Refrigerate for up to 10 days. Freeze for up to 6 months.

### TIPS & VARIATIONS

- **Mole and many dried chile-based recipes will always be more flavorful the next day.**
- **Different dried chiles will yield a different color mole.**
- **If you don't want to use lard, a neutral oil of your choice will work.**
- **If you prefer not to use peanuts due to allergies, just bump up the quantity of the other nuts and seeds.**
- **This recipe can easily accommodate 12 to 14 chicken pieces. Add them to the mole after it has simmered for 2 hours, then simmer 1 hour more.**

# Caldillo de Jitomate

A cross between a salsa and a sauce, this easy, tomato-based *caldillo* sauce is delicious for *chiles rellenos*, *entomatadas*, and *queso en salsa*. For those days when you don't want to commit to a spicy blended salsa, this one will enhance the flavor profile of your favorite Mexican dishes. Serve warm *caldillo* over *chiles rellenos*, *taquitos*, or tacos *dorados*.

PREP TIME: **15 MINUTES**
COOK TIME: **30 MINUTES**
YIELD: **3½ CUPS**

1 pound (about 5) Roma tomatoes

1 serrano pepper, coarsely chopped

3 *arbol* peppers

¼ medium white onion

3 cloves garlic

2 teaspoons tomato or chicken bouillon

Freshly ground pepper, to taste

Pinch of oregano

Salt, to taste

1½ tablespoons avocado oil

In a saucepan over medium heat, bring 4 cups of water to a simmer.

With a small, sharp knife, slice an X on the bottom of the tomatoes. Transfer the tomatoes, peppers, onion, and garlic to the simmering water. Cook for 10 minutes.

Remove the tomatoes from the water, reserving the liquid, and carefully peel away the skin and discard it. Place the tomatoes, peppers, onion, and garlic in a blender jar along with 2 cups of the reserved cooking water. Add the bouillon, pepper, oregano, and salt, to taste. Blend on high until smooth.

Heat the oil in a saucepan over medium heat for 3 minutes. Once hot, add the *caldillo* sauce from the blender jar. Stir well. Cook at a steady simmer for 15 to 20 minutes. Taste for seasoning. Store in glass jars refrigerated for up to 10 days.

TIPS & VARIATIONS

- **Double the recipe and drop Mexican-style meatballs (*albondigas*) into the sauce. Simmer for 25 minutes, stirring after 10 minutes. Serve as an appetizer or with rice, beans, and tortillas as a main meal.**
- **Use tomatillos instead of tomatoes and 4 serrano peppers in place of the 3 *chile de arbol* peppers. Follow the instructions as written, except there is no need to peel the tomatillos.**

# Adobo Verde

There are so many variations for *adobo rojo*, but not enough that use fresh green chile peppers, herbs, and spices. This *adobo verde* can be used for chicken, pork, seafood, and vegetables. My best suggestion is to prepare the adobo a few days ahead for the richest flavor.

PREP TIME: **30 MINUTES**
COOK TIME: **35 MINUTES**
YIELD: **2½ CUPS**

8 large serrano peppers

10 cloves garlic, skin on

1 large bunch of cilantro, stemmed

1 large bunch of flat-leaf parsley, stemmed

1 teaspoon dried thyme

1 teaspoon dried marjoram

1 teaspoon cumin

1½ tablespoons fresh oregano leaves or 2 teaspoons dried oregano

¼ cup fresh lime juice (2 large limes)

¼ cup apple cider vinegar

1¼ cups avocado or olive oil

Salt and pepper, to taste

Dry roast the peppers on a griddle or skillet along with the cloves of garlic over medium heat. After a few minutes, the peppers will start to crackle and blister. Turn the peppers and garlic as needed for the next 15 minutes. Remove the skin from the garlic.

To the blender, add the roasted serrano peppers, peeled garlic, cilantro, parsley, thyme, marjoram, cumin, oregano, lime juice, vinegar, and oil. Season with salt and pepper. Blend on high until smooth. Taste again for salt.

Store in glass jars refrigerated for several months.

TIPS & VARIATIONS

- **Use the adobo to marinate chicken, pork, lamb, or beef. Cook the meat in a hot skillet, add sliced onion and garlic, and serve as a taco filling. Garnish with cilantro, lime, and avocado.**
- **Mix in a few tablespoons during the last 10 minutes of roasting vegetables.**
- **Add a few tablespoons of the adobo to Greek yogurt or sour cream for a vegetable dip.**

# Cochinita Pibil Adobo

*Cochinita pibil* is a pork dish especially popular in Yucatán. The bright-red marinade or adobo is prepared with *achiote* paste, spices, and bitter orange juice. A traditional pork *pibil* is pork wrapped in banana leaves and roasted for hours in an underground oven. The adobo is distinct in color and flavor.

**PREP TIME: 20 MINUTES**
**COOK TIME: 8 MINUTES**
**YIELD: 2¼ CUPS**

- 2 teaspoons cumin seeds
- 2 teaspoons peppercorns
- 2 teaspoons Mexican oregano
- 1 teaspoon coriander seeds
- 1 teaspoon crushed *arbol* or *piquin* peppers (optional)
- 1-inch piece Mexican cinnamon stick
- 1½ cups fresh orange juice (6 large oranges)
- ½ cup fresh lime juice (4 limes)
- ⅓ cup extra-virgin olive oil
- ¼ cup *achiote* paste, chopped
- 6 cloves garlic, minced
- ½ medium white onion, chopped
- Salt, to taste

Over medium heat, in a dry skillet, combine the cumin, peppercorns, oregano, coriander seeds, peppers (if using), and cinnamon. Stirring now and then, toast for 5 to 7 minutes, or until the spices become aromatic.

Transfer the spice mixture to a blender jar. Add the orange juice, lime juice, oil, *achiote* paste, garlic, and onion. Blend on high until very smooth, scraping down the sides as needed. Season with salt.

Store the adobo for 2 days to intensify and marry all the flavors. Or you can use it right away to marinate up to an 8-pound pork shoulder roast or two 4-pound roaster whole chickens. Store in glass jars refrigerated for up to 14 days. Freeze for up to 6 months.

### TIPS & VARIATIONS

- **If you can find the traditional sour or bitter oranges favored in Mexico, use them to achieve an authentic flavor. Omit the regular oranges and limes. In some Hispanic markets, you can find a bitter-orange marinade that works great in a pinch.**
- ***Achiote*** **paste is produced when bright-red, ground annatto seeds are ground with spices. It is used in many traditional Yucatan dishes. I bumped up the flavors here by adding additional spices, onion, and garlic. The quantity given is good for up to 10 pounds of pork shoulder or butt.**

# Birria Adobo

*Birria* is a traditional dish prepared with goat and popular in Jalisco, Mexico. For most of us, goat meat is not readily available, and beef is a popular and delicious alternative. The adobo, depending on the region of Mexico, varies and may or may not include tomatoes.

PREP TIME: **25 MINUTES**
COOK TIME: **22 MINUTES**
YIELD: **6 CUPS**

3 tablespoons avocado oil
1 small white onion, sliced
6 cloves garlic
2-inch piece of fresh ginger, roughly chopped
1 large Roma tomato, quartered
9 California chile pods, seeded and stemmed
5 *morita* chile pods, seeds included
1 teaspoon peppercorns
1 teaspoon cumin seeds
1 teaspoon marjoram
1 teaspoon thyme
4 whole cloves
1-inch Mexican cinnamon stick
Salt, to taste

In a large pot, preheat the oil over medium heat for 1 minute. Add the onion, garlic, ginger, and tomato. Sauté for 8 minutes. Add the chile pods and sauté for 3 minutes more. Finally, add the peppercorns, cumin seeds, marjoram, thyme, cloves, and cinnamon and cook for 1 minute more.

Pour in 4½ cups of water to cover the mixture. Bring to a simmer and cook for 10 minutes. Using a slotted spoon, transfer the softened ingredients to a blender jar. Next, pour in the liquid. Season with salt. Blend on high until smooth. If you are not using a power blender, strain the adobo through a fine-mesh sieve into a bowl.

Transfer to glass jars. Store refrigerated for 1 month or freeze for up to 6 months.

This adobo is enough to prepare 6 pounds of beef chuck roast and ribs combined.

## TIPS & VARIATIONS

- **There are two ways to prepare *birria* in a home kitchen. The first is to marinate the beef overnight with the adobo. On the next day, let the beef in the adobo come up to room temperature, then pour enough water into the pot to cover the beef generously. Bring to a boil over medium heat. Cover partially and continue cooking for 3 to 3½ hours, or until the beef falls apart easily.**
- **The second way is to sear the seasoned beef in a large pot with onion and garlic, then cover with water. Bring to a boil, reduce the heat, and then pour in the *birria* adobo. Continue cooking for 3 to 3½ hours, or until the beef is very tender.**

# Pollo Adobado

This delicious *pollo adobado* is inspired by beer-can chicken. It is especially juicy and tender, with the flavors of the Yucatan. The easy homemade adobo prepared with *recado rojo* is fresh and simple to prepare. Combine these fresh ingredients with that vibrant red *achiote*, and you are all set!

The *achiote* paste, or *recado*, is readily available in most Mexican markets and online.

PREP TIME: **25 MINUTES**
COOK TIME: **3 HOURS**
YIELD: **6 SERVINGS**

¼ cup fresh orange juice (2 large oranges), plus 1 orange, sliced into rings

¼ cup fresh lemon juice (2 lemons), plus 1 lemon, sliced into rings

6 cloves garlic

¼ cup *achiote* paste

1 teaspoon cumin

1 teaspoon oregano

3 teaspoons freshly ground pepper, plus more to taste

3 teaspoons salt, plus more to taste

⅓ cup avocado oil

6 pounds whole broiler chicken

One 12-ounce can of beer

1 large onion, sliced

2 serrano peppers, sliced

1 teaspoon dried thyme

In a blender, add the orange juice, lemon juice, 3 cloves of the garlic, the *achiote* paste, cumin, oregano, pepper, salt, and oil. Blend on high until very smooth, then divide equally into two bowls. Set aside.

Clean the chicken and rinse it under cold water. Pat dry with paper towels. Season the inside and outside with salt and pepper. Let stand at room temperature for 45 minutes to 1 hour.

Preheat the oven to 350°F. In the bottom of a roasting pan, place the rack for the chicken in the center. Add 3 tablespoons of adobo into the cavity of the chicken.

Pour half of the beer into the bottom of the roasting pan. Place the can with the remaining beer in the center of the rack. Carefully stand the chicken over the can and secure it so it feels centered. In the bottom of the roasting pan, add 2 cups of water and the onion, the reserved 3 cloves of garlic, the sliced orange, sliced lemon, serrano peppers, thyme, and salt and pepper to taste.

Using the remaining adobo from the same bowl, brush the whole chicken generously. If there is any adobo left in the bowl, pour it into the bottom of the roasting pan. Tent the chicken with aluminum foil and carefully transfer it to the preheated oven. Roast for 90 minutes, rotating the pan halfway through.

After 90 minutes, remove the foil. Take the second bowl of adobo and baste the whole chicken once again. Return to the oven and continue roasting for another 40 to 60 minutes. After 20 minutes, baste the chicken 1 to 2 more times. The chicken is done when the internal temperature reaches 165°F. Remove it from the oven and let stand for 25 minutes. Strain the sauce at the bottom of the roasting pan and spoon it over the chicken to add moisture and more flavor. Serve and enjoy!

### TIPS & VARIATIONS

- **You can prepare this recipe faster if you butterfly the chicken and lay it skin-side up on a baking sheet or in a roasting pan with a rack. After seasoning and basting with the adobo, roast at 450°F until the internal temperature of the thigh reaches 165°F. Depending on the size of the roaster, it will take 45 minutes to 1 hour.**

# Beef Birria

Cocula, Jalisco, is said to be the birthplace of *birria* prepared with goat. *Birria* is the term used in Jalisco to describe meats cooked in a pit or earth oven. In other parts of Mexico, this method is called *barbacoa*. Home cooks in Mexico became enamored of the beef version of this dish and it is now very popular around the country. Serve with warm corn tortillas.

PREP TIME: **40 MINUTES**
COOK TIME: **3 HOURS, 30 MINUTES**
YIELD: **6 SERVINGS**

**BEEF**

3 pounds chuck roast, cut into large chunks

Salt and pepper, to taste

4 tablespoons avocado or extra-virgin olive oil

½ large white onion

5 cloves garlic

3 bay leaves

1 cup dried chickpeas, soaked in water for several hours, or canned chickpeas

**SAUCE**

9 California chile pods

4 *morita* chile pods

3 tablespoons avocado oil

1 large white onion (½ for beef; ½ in strips, for sauce)

10 cloves garlic (5 cloves for beef, 5 for sauce)

2-inch piece of fresh ginger, peeled and roughly chopped

1 large Roma tomato, quartered

1 teaspoon peppercorns

1 teaspoon cumin seeds

1 teaspoon marjoram

1 teaspoon thyme

4 whole cloves

1-inch cinnamon stick

Salt, to taste

**GARNISH**

1 cup finely chopped onion

½ cup minced cilantro

4 limes, sliced into wedges

¾ cup Spicy Birria Salsa (page 63)

Slice the beef into large chunks and transfer to a large baking sheet. Season the beef lightly with salt and pepper all around. Let the beef sit at room temperature for 35 minutes. After 35 minutes, preheat the oil at medium heat for 3 minutes. After 3 minutes, sear and brown the beef for 5 minutes per side. Turn as needed. Add ¼ of the onion and the garlic. Saute for 3 minutes. Carefully, pour into the pot 1 gallon of water. Stir gently. Season with salt, to taste. Add bay leaves and soaked chickpeas. Bring up to a light boil and skim off the foam on top as needed. Cook at a steady simmer for 90 minutes.

continues on page 114

continued from page 112

Remove the stems and seeds from large pods. *Chile morita* typically comes with no stems. I leave the seeds in to add heat to the recipe.

In a separate large pot, preheat the oil to medium heat for 1 minute. Add the remaining ¼ cup onion, plus the garlic, ginger, and tomato. Sauté for a few minutes. Add the chile pods and sauté for another 4 minutes. Add the peppercorns, cumin seeds, marjoram, thyme, cloves, and cinnamon. Stir to combine and sauté for 1 more minute.

To the pot with the chiles, pour about 4 cups of water. Bring up to a simmer and cook for 10 minutes. Using a slotted spoon or tongs, transfer softened ingredients to the blender. Then pour in all the liquid with spices. Season with salt. Blend on high until smooth. Taste for salt. Strain half of the chile sauce through a wire fine-mesh strainer directly into the pot with the simmering beef. Strain the remaining sauce and store in the freezer for up to 6 months for when you prepare *birria* again.

After 90 minutes, remove and discard the onion, garlic, and bay leaves from the pot where you cooked the beef. Continue cooking *birria* until beef is very tender. This could take another 60 minutes. To serve, add some beef to each bowl, then ladle in some of the consommé. Garnish with the onion, cilantro, a squeeze of lime, and the salsa.

## TIPS & VARIATIONS

- **Traditional *birria is* prepared with goat meat, but can be adapted using beef, pork, and even chicken. For a lighter consommé, you omit the tomato and half of the California chile pods.**
- **To prepare *quesa birria* tacos, skim the fat from the cooked *birria* in the pot. Brush or dip corn tortillas in the fat and place on a preheated skillet. Add ¼ cup of a good melting cheese, such as Chihuahua, and add some of the shredded *birria* meat. Fold over like a taco and continue cooking, turning as needed, until the tortillas become darker in color and slightly crisp around the edges. Serve the tacos with some of the consommé on the side. Dip and enjoy!**

# Chile Colorado Pork Tamal

The word "*colorado*" describes the red, dried chiles used in this recipe. This is the tamale recipe that I remember most from my childhood. The only change I made to it is that I use *masa harina* to prepare the *masa* because that is what is available to me. These tamales are also known as *tamales norteños* and are popular in Nuevo Leon, Mexico.

PREP TIME: **1 HOUR, 30 MINUTES**
COOK TIME: **4 HOURS, 30 MINUTES**
YIELD: **48 MEDIUM TAMALES**

**PORK**

4½ pounds boneless pork butt or shoulder

1 tablespoon coarse salt

1 large white onion, sliced

2 whole garlic bulbs, sliced open

4 bay leaves

**TAMALES**

60 corn husks for medium tamales, soaked (48 for tamales, 12 for steaming the tamales)

¼ cup of naturally rendered pork lard

***CHILE ANCHO* SALSA/SAUCE (SEE RECIPE *MASA* FOR TAMALES)**

1¾ cups naturally rendered pork lard, at room temperature

3 teaspoons baking powder

3 teaspoons salt

5 cups *masa harina* (instant corn flour) for tamales

4 cups pork broth, room temperature, from the cooked pork

1 cup Chile Ancho Salsa (page 99), at room temperature

20-quart steamer pot

Slice the pork into 3-inch chunks, then transfer it to a large pot. Cover the pork with 4 liters of water. Add the salt, onion, garlic, and bay leaves. At medium-high heat, bring the pork up to a boil. Reduce the heat and continue cooking at a steady simmer for 3 hours, or until the pork is tender. Skim the foam off the top as needed. Flip the pork over halfway through the cooking time.

Place the corn husk in a large pot and cover with boiling water. Cover and soak for a few hours. Prepare the *ancho* salsa while the pork cooks. Reserve 1 cup of the sauce to prepare the *masa*. See recipe.

Once the pork is tender, remove the pork from the broth. Chop the pork roughly. Cover and set it aside. Reserve all of the broth. Preheat ¼ cup of the naturally rendered pork lard to medium heat in a large pot for 4 minutes. Once it is hot, carefully pour in the salsa. It will boil

continues on page 117

continued from page 115

rapidly, so have the lid handy. Stir and cook the sauce for 10 minutes. After 10 minutes, add all the chopped pork. Cook at a low simmer for 45 minutes to 1 hour or until it reduces and thickens. Taste for salt. Let the pork cool completely before filling the tamales.

### CORN MASA

In the bowl of the stand mixer, whip the lard for 3 minutes. Mix in the baking powder and salt. Mix for 1 more minute. Gradually mix in the *masa harina* instant corn flour. Mix in the 1 cup of reserved *chile ancho* sauce. Gradually mix in 4 cups of reserved pork broth. Mix at a medium speed for 10 minutes. You will adjust the salt as you mix the *masa*. It should taste a little salty. The *masa* should have a frosting-like texture and be easy to spread. If the *masa* is too thick, mix in a little more of the reserved broth. If it is too loose, mix in a little more *masa harina*. Keep *masa* covered with a damp paper towel or plastic wrap until ready to use. Store it in the refrigerator for up to two days if you are not using it right away.

### ASSEMBLE TAMALES

Shake off excess water from corn husks. Tear the husks so they are all even, about 5½ inches wide. Place the corn husk in the palm of your hand with the wide side closest to you. Spread about 4 to 5 tablespoons of *masa* all over the bottom half of the husk. Place 3 tablespoons of pork filling down the center of the tamal. Fold in the sides to cover the meat filling (it should overlap a little on the first fold). Fold down the top flap down and lay tamale seam-side down until ready to cook.

### STEAM TAMALES

Fill the bottom of a large 20-quart steamer pot with water ½ inch below the indicated line. Insert the steamer. Tear a few of the extra corn husks into thin strips and place on top of the steamer insert. Arrange all your tamales standing up (open-side up). Take a few extra corn husks and arrange them on top of the filled tamales. This will help keep them moist while they steam. It will also prevent water from going into the filled tamales. Turn heat to high. Once they begin to steam rapidly, then reduce the heat to medium. Set the timer to 1 hour. After 1 hour, carefully remove one tamal and let it cool on a plate for 3 minutes. If the husk comes away easily, the tamales are ready. If not, continue steaming for 30 more minutes. The *masa* will firm up as the tamales cool. Serve as is or with your favorite salsa. Once tamales cool, store them in large plastic storage bags. Tamales will keep in the refrigerator for 10 to 12 days.

### TIPS & VARIATIONS

- **My best advice is to break down the recipe into two or three days. The sauce will become more flavorful prepared one day ahead. The meat with the sauce is also more flavorful if it sits for 24 hours overnight. Freeze uncooked tamales for up to 3 months. Tamales prepared from *masa harina* will tend to dry out if you freeze them cooked. Whenever possible, purchase fresh ground *masa* from the local tortilla factory or Mexican Market.**

# Enchiladas Rojas

In my family, enchiladas were prepared with corn tortillas that were lightly fried, filled, then tightly rolled. They were plated, topped with warm enchilada sauce, and garnished with crumbled cheese. The fillings were simply shredded chicken or a crumbled *queso fresco* mixed with chopped onions. This is the family-style baked version with lots of melted cheese on top.

PREP TIME: **40 MINUTES**
COOK TIME: **1 HOUR, 50 MINUTES**
YIELD: **6 SERVINGS**

- 2 pounds boneless chicken breasts or 5 boneless thighs
- 1 teaspoon salt, plus more to taste
- 2 *ancho* chile peppers
- 9 *guajillo* chile peppers
- 4 *arbol* chile peppers
- 1 large Roma tomato, halved
- ½ medium white onion, quartered
- 3 cloves garlic
- ¼ cup avocado or olive oil
- 1 teaspoon Mexican oregano
- 1 teaspoon cumin seeds
- 1 teaspoon peppercorns
- 16 corn tortillas
- Avocado or canola oil
- 8 ounces Monterey Jack or Chihuahua cheese, shredded

In a large pot, cover the chicken with 6 cups of water. Season with salt. Bring to a boil over medium heat. When the chicken begins to boil, reduce the heat to medium-low. Simmer for 35 to 40 minutes. Skim the foam off the top as needed. Remove the chicken from the pot and shred it while it is still warm. Cover and set it aside. Reserve the stock for the enchilada sauce.

Combine the chile peppers, tomato, onion, and garlic in a medium saucepan. Drizzle with 1½ tablespoons of the oil and heat to medium. Sauté for 5 minutes, stirring often.

Cover with 4 cups of the reserved stock. Bring to a boil, then reduce the heat, and cook until the tomatoes are tender and the peppers are soft. Let stand for 10 minutes.

Using tongs, transfer all the solids to a blender first. Carefully pour in all the stock from the pan. Add the oregano, cumin, and peppercorns, and season with salt. Pour in 1 cup of the reserved stock. If there isn't enough, add water. Blend on high until smooth. Taste for salt.

In the same pan you cooked the peppers, add 2 tablespoons of oil and heat over medium heat for 2 minutes. Strain the sauce through a wire-mesh sieve directly into the pot with the hot oil. Bring to a boil, reduce to a simmer, and continue cooking for 15 to 20 minutes.

#### FOR FAMILY-STYLE

In a 9-by-13-inch pan, spread 1 cup of enchilada sauce evenly to cover the bottom of the pan. Set aside.

In a skillet, preheat ½ cup of oil over medium heat for 3 to 4 minutes. When the oil is hot, fry the tortillas for 15 to 20 seconds per side to soften them. Stack the softened tortillas on a plate and cover with foil.

In a bowl, combine the shredded chicken breast with ½ cup of enchilada sauce, and stir well to combine. Fill the tortillas with 2 tablespoons of the chicken and roll them as tightly as you can so they resemble little flutes. Lay the enchiladas in the baking pan with the sauce already in it. Once you have filled and rolled all the enchiladas, top them with the remaining sauce and shredded cheese. Bake in a preheated 350°F oven for 25 minutes.

#### TIPS & VARIATIONS

- **For the traditional version of this dish, dip the tortillas in the enchilada sauce and fry them in shallow oil. This will sear the sauce into the tortillas.**
- **Carefully fill and roll them or fold them over like a taco. Garnish with crumbled *queso fresco* and Mexican *crema*. Garnishes included fried carrots and potatoes coated with enchilada sauce, shredded lettuce, thinly sliced onion, sliced tomato, avocado slices, and a spicy salsa.**

# Taqueria–La Taquiza

## TACO PARTY

Welcome to the vibrant heart of the taqueria, where the sizzle of the griddle and the aroma of fresh tortillas fill the air! In this chapter, we're bringing the fiesta to your kitchen with a collection of classic taqueria delights, from the essential Guacamole y Totopos (page 133) to the irresistible Tacos Gobernador (page 145) shrimp tacos.

We'll master the art of making the perfect taco, with options like crispy Tacos Dorados de Picadillo (page 142), flavorful Bistec en Salsa (page 138), and slow-cooked Cochinita Pibil Panuchos (page 148). But it's not just about the fillings. We'll also explore the sides that make a taquiza complete, like tangy Pickled Red Onions (page 127), fiery Chiles Toreados & Cebollitas (page 124), and the perfect Tricolored Corn Tortillas (page 131). Get ready to roll up your sleeves and create a taqueria experience that's truly unforgettable!

# Escabeche

*Escabeche* is the Spanish word used to describe vegetables or meats that are pickled or marinated. My first experience with *escabeche* was as a kid. Mom's easy version consisted of sautéed or poached slices of jalapeño peppers and carrots.

She would place them in a large container, then open a big can of store-bought pickled jalapeño peppers and pour the entire contents of the can over the jalapeño peppers and carrots. Sometimes, she would add chunks of peeled, cooked potatoes. She would cover the container tightly and let the vegetables sit for a few days. My version of *chiles en escabeche* is prepared from scratch.

PREP TIME: **20 MINUTES**
COOK TIME: **20 MINUTES**
YIELD: **48 OUNCES**

3½ tablespoons avocado oil

4 carrots, peeled and sliced into ½-inch rings

12 jalapeño peppers, stemmed and sliced into ½-inch rings

1 medium white onion, thinly sliced

2 cups distilled white vinegar

4 cloves garlic

1 tablespoon oregano

4 bay leaves

Salt, to taste

In a large skillet over medium heat, add the oil. After 1 minute, add the carrots. Sauté the carrots for 3 minutes. Add the jalapeño peppers and onion. Sauté for another 3 minutes.

In a small bowl, mix the vinegar with 2 cups of water. Season with salt. The mixture must be a little salty to season the vegetables properly. Set aside.

Add the garlic, oregano, and bay leaves to the skillet. Sauté for 1 minute. Pour in the vinegar-and-water mixture. Stir to combine. Bring the *escabeche* to a light simmer over low heat and cook for 6 minutes. Remove it from the heat and let the *escabeche* cool to room temperature.

Store in glass jars in the refrigerator for 3 months.

TIPS & VARIATIONS

- **Store filled jars in the coldest part of the refrigerator. Pour out the portion you want to use and return the jar to the refrigerator. Constant temperature change will cause the *escabeche* to change flavor and become sour.**
- **Omit the jalapeño peppers and substitute other fresh chile peppers, such as serrano, habanero, Fresno, cayenne, caribe (*güero*), or Manzano peppers.**
- **Add a mix of vegetables such as cauliflower, green beans, or baby potatoes. Poach them first in simmering water. The potatoes must be fork-tender and cooked through before adding them to the *escabeche*.**

# Chiles Toreados & Cebollitas

No *carne asada* day would be complete without *chiles toreados* and *cebollitas* (knob onions) on the side! "*Toreados*" is a Mexican cooking technique in which fresh chile peppers are fried, pan seared, or grilled until the skin is blistered and charred. Grilled or pan-seared knob onions go hand in hand with them for the complete taco experience!

PREP TIME: **10 MINUTES**
COOK TIME: **35 MINUTES**
YIELD: **6 SERVINGS**

- 6 jalapeño peppers
- 6 serrano peppers
- 6 *güero* (caribe) peppers
- ¾ cup avocado oil
- 6 knob onions
- ¼ cup fresh lime juice (2 large limes)
- ½ cup soy sauce
- Salt, to taste

Wash and dry the chile peppers. Take 1 chile pepper at a time and gently roll it using both hands to loosen the seeds and membranes inside the peppers. This will release the capsicum inside, making the peppers spicier. Using a small, sharp knife, slice a small slit on the tip of each pepper. Set them aside.

In a deep skillet, pour in the oil. Heat over medium heat for 3 minutes.

In the meantime, trim the green parts of the knob onions off; trim the tops so they are flat.

Once the oil is hot, add all the chile peppers. Be careful because the oil will pop as it contacts the moisture from the peppers. You want the skin to blacken and blister all around. Turn them as needed. If the peppers are burning too quickly, reduce the heat slightly.

Remove the blistered peppers and transfer them to a large shallow serving dish. Pour out into a heatproof bowl, leaving most of the oil in the skillet. Save it for future cooking.

Over medium heat, place the knob onions in the skillet. Fry them for 15 minutes, turning as needed, then remove from the skillet.

In a small bowl, combine the onions and chile peppers. Squeeze the fresh lime juice evenly over the onions and peppers. Pour in the soy sauce. Gently mix. If needed, season with salt. Serve right away.

### TIPS & VARIATIONS

- **Prepare a *chile toreado* appetizer. Take the larger cooked jalapeño peppers and *güeros* and stuff them with cooked, seasoned, and chopped shrimp. Garnish plate with thinly sliced red onions and cucumbers.**
- **Use *chiles torteados* in your favorite salsa and guacamole recipes. They add a whole extra level of roasted flavor that is delicious!**

# Pickled Red Onions

These simple pickled red onions are one of the most popular recipe requests I get when they're posted in my food photos. *Curtido* is the name in Spanish. The always popular Yucatan dish of pork *cochinita pibil* would not be the same without the signature habanero pickled red onions.

PREP TIME: **30 MINUTES**
COOK TIME: **35 MINUTES**
YIELD: **2½ CUPS**

1 extra-large red onion, thinly sliced

2 habanero peppers, thinly sliced

1 teaspoon crushed Mexican oregano

2 tablespoons fresh lime juice (1 large lime)

⅓ cup distilled white vinegar

Salt, to taste

Combine all the ingredients in a bowl, then toss well to combine. Cover and let sit for 1 hour, stirring occasionally.

Transfer the mixture to glass jars and chill until ready to serve. Store refrigerated for up to 2 weeks.

TIPS & VARIATIONS

- **If you want the onions to be less acidic, replace some of the vinegar with cold water. Mix in 1 tablespoon of agave syrup.**
- **The *curtido* can be prepared with any variety of fresh chiles and some smaller dried chile pepper varieties, such as *arbol* peppers, *piquin*, and *chiltepin*.**

# Tortillas Taqueras de Harina

**What is the ideal size for a flour tortilla? In my journey learning to prepare flour tortillas from scratch, my goal has always been larger and thinner! But, on occasion, I love, love, love a smaller, thicker flour tortilla to wrap around my favorite fillings!**

**PREP TIME: 50 MINUTES**
**COOK TIME: 25 MINUTES**
**YIELD: 16 TORTILLAS**

**3½ cups unbleached flour, sifted, plus more for dredging**

**1 teaspoon salt**

**¼ cup pork lard, butter, shortening, or avocado oil, at room temperature**

**1½ tablespoons shortening**

In a large bowl, mix the flour and salt. Using a pastry cutter or with clean hands, cut the soft lard or butter into the flour and salt until the mixture resembles small crumbs.

Gradually mix in 1½ cups of lukewarm water, ¼ cup at a time, mixing well between each addition. I use almost the full amount of water, but you may need to add more or less to reach the desired consistency. Different flour brands may yield slightly different results. Humidity and elevation, too, play a part in the amount of water needed. The dough should feel sticky, but manageable.

Transfer the dough to a flat surface and knead it aggressively for 5 to 7 minutes until it becomes mostly smooth. Cover it with plastic wrap and let it rest for 10 to 15 minutes.

Form the dough into 16 equal-size balls and place them on a large baking sheet. Rub the shortening between the palms of your hands and rub a light coating on the tops of the balls, flattening them slightly. Cover again and let rest for 10 to 15 minutes.

Preheat a griddle to medium-low.

One by one, dredge the dough balls in flour. Place the first ball on a flat surface and begin to roll it forward, then back. Rotate it slightly and repeat. If the tortilla sticks, sprinkle with flour. Continue until you reach a tortilla that measures about 6½ inches. Repeat for the remaining dough balls.

Place the flattened tortilla on the hot griddle. Bubbles should start to form within a few seconds. If they form too fast, the griddle may be too hot. If they take too long to form, the griddle may not be hot enough. Adjust the heat accordingly.

Flip the tortilla and cook it on the other side for 25 to 30 seconds. Flip again and you should see it inflate. I use a flat-edge wooden spatula to gently press the edges of the tortilla, encouraging it to inflate further. Continue until all the tortillas are cooked, then stack them in a tortilla warmer lined with a dish towel. Enjoy them while they are still warm.

For any leftover tortillas, lay them on a dish towel to dry out for 10 minutes. Stack and wrap them in a dish towel and place them in a plastic food bag. Refrigerate for up to 10 days. When ready to use them, reheat them on a hot griddle for 25 to 30 seconds per side.

### TIPS & VARIATIONS

- **If using butter, I suggest using Irish butter because, unlike most brands of butter, it contains no water, which yields a better tortilla. Rendered bacon fat works great too!**
- **Use this same recipe to roll out a larger and thinner 8-inch flour tortilla.**

# Tricolored Corn Tortillas

I enjoy a good challenge in the kitchen. So, I was thrilled to take on this fun project to honor Mexico's Independence Day: create a recipe for tricolored corn tortillas. My dad, Ramiro, instilled his love of the corn tortilla in my siblings and me, so I was well versed in making that staple Mexican food. And, as luck would have it, I could use natural ingredients to add the vibrant colors I wanted.

PREP TIME: **1 HOUR, 45 MINUTES**
COOK TIME: **1 HOUR, 30 MINUTES**
YIELD: **45 TORTILLAS**

**GREEN CORN *MASA***

1 cup fresh kale, stemmed

3¾ cups instant corn-flour *masa harina*

**RED CORN *MASA***

8 dried *guajillo* pepper pods, seeded and stemmed

3¾ cups instant corn-flour *masa harina*

**REGULAR *MASA***

2 cups water, lukewarm

3 cups instant corn-flour *masa harina*

**GREEN CORN MASA**

Tear the kale into pieces and transfer them to the blender. Add 2 cups of lukewarm water and blend on high until smooth. Discard any foam on top.

Pour the liquid into a bowl and gradually mix in the corn-flour *masa harina* to form a dough. If the dough is sticky, continue mixing in *masa harina* until you achieve a modeling claylike consistency. The mixture should not stick to your hands. Cover the bowl with plastic wrap and set aside.

Check the dough after 10 minutes. If it feels sticky, mix in a little more *masa harina*, then wrap the *masa* tightly in plastic wrap. Leave at room temperature while you mix the other colors.

**RED CORN MASA**

Add the *guajillo* peppers to 4 cups of simmering water. Cook for 6 minutes. Remove from the heat and let sit for 10 minutes before draining the water. Transfer the chiles to a blender. Pour in 2 cups of lukewarm water and blend on high until very smooth.

continues on page 132

continued from page 131

Pour the chile mixture into a large bowl. Gradually mix in the *masa harina* until the dough comes together and is no longer sticky. Roll a ball of *masa* in your hands. If you can press your finger in the center and don't see any cracks around the edges, then the *masa* is fully hydrated. Repeat the instructions from the green *masa*.

**REGULAR MASA**

Pour 2 cups of lukewarm water into a large bowl. Gradually mix in the *masa harina* until the dough comes together. If any of the *masa* feels dry, mix in a little more water. Too sticky, mix in a little more *masa harina*. Form into a log, wrap in plastic wrap, and let sit for 10 minutes before using.

For a 4-inch corn tortilla, you want to weigh out ¼ to ⅓ ounces of each color of *masa*. Roll in between the palms of your hands until it resembles a short, skinny cigar. Lay the colors green, white, and red side by side on a lined tortilla press. Press gently at first, then harder, until you reach the desired thickness. I used a small press so I couldn't go wider than 4½ inches.

On a large nonstick griddle preheated to medium heat, lay the pressed tortilla down. Let it cook for 15 seconds or until it releases easily. Flip and cook for 30 seconds, then flip again. Flip a third time. The tortilla should inflate at this point. Cook for 15 seconds.

Transfer the cooked tortillas into a large tortilla warmer that is lined with a light dish towel. The steam created will yield a soft flexible tortilla.

To reheat, preheat the griddle until it is very hot. Heat each tortilla, turning as needed. As soon as each softens, transfer it to a covered tortilla warmer to steam a little.

TIPS & VARIATIONS

- **I don't recommend freezing the *masa* because it will dry out.**
- **Other ingredients that can add color to tortillas are beets, carrots, poblanos, cactus, cilantro, red jalapeño peppers, turmeric, annatto powder, and good-quality chili powders.**
- **If your tortillas don't inflate, there's a chance they may have been overcooked on the first side. The *masa* needs to be fully hydrated and the temperature on the griddle should be hot, but not smoking. If they stick, bubble up in spots, and burn on one side, the surface is probably too hot. The first couple of tortillas are typically testers.**
- **When the tortillas are still a bit warm and pliable is the best time to fill and roll them for *taquitos*, tacos *dorados*, or enchiladas. Lay the filled tortillas seam-side down, side by side, for 10 to 15 minutes. Fry lightly for enchiladas; fry until crunchy for *taquitos* and tacos *dorados*.**

# Guacamole y Totopos

My earliest memories of enjoying guacamole and *totopos* are as a very young child. I wanted to eat guacamole for breakfast, lunch, and dinner! When I was teaching cooking classes, the students were often surprised at how delicious the fresh-made guacamole with homemade chips (*totopos*) were compared to the average Mexican restaurant.

PREP TIME: **35 MINUTES**
COOK TIME: **35 MINUTES**
YIELD: **6 SERVINGS**

**TOTOPOS**

25 corn tortillas (6-inch round)

2½ cups canola oil

Sea salt, to taste

**GUACAMOLE**

½ teaspoon salt, plus more to taste

2 cloves garlic

2 serrano peppers, stemmed and coarsely chopped

Handful of fresh cilantro, coarsely chopped

2 large, ripe avocados, peeled and pitted

2 Roma tomatoes, finely chopped

½ cup finely chopped onion

2 tablespoons fresh lime juice (1 large lime)

### TOTOPOS

Slice the tortillas into 6 equal wedges. Set them aside.

In a large, heavy pot over medium heat, preheat the oil for 15 minutes. Line a baking sheet with paper towels.

Fry the tortillas in batches until crispy. Turn as needed. Drain crispy chips onto the baking sheet and season lightly with salt. Yields 1½ pounds. Store chips in a airtight bag for up to 10 days.

### GUACAMOLE

In a *molcajete*, smash and grind the salt and garlic into a fine paste. Repeat with the peppers and cilantro. Spoon in the avocado, gently mixing. Once creamy, combine with a small wooden spoon. Mix in the tomato, onion, and lime juice. Stir, taste for salt. Serve with fresh *totopos*!

### TIPS & VARIATIONS

- **Get creative with your guacamole and serve these extras on the side! Toasted *pepitas*, minced radishes, pomegranate seeds, crumbled bacon, crumbled *cotija* or feta cheese, grilled shrimp, or grilled corn! So many possibilities!**

# Enchiladas de Queso

On most days, I really do prefer my enchiladas with no sauce. I like them with just a bit of extra *queso fresco* and onion. While in Monterrey, I always stop at Taqueria Juarez, where I order a delicious combo plate that includes enchiladas *de queso*. These are corn tortillas infused with a red chile sauce. The side of chunky fried potatoes is traditional and fantastic!

**PREP TIME: 35 MINUTES**
**COOK TIME: 40 MINUTES**
**YIELD: 4 SERVINGS**

**CHIPOTLE *CREMA***

1 cup Mexican *crema* or sour cream

½ teaspoon chipotle powder or 1 chipotle in adobo, minced

⅓ teaspoon smoked paprika

2 tablespoons fresh lime juice (1 large lime)

¼ cup cold water or milk to thin out the *crema*

Salt, to taste

**POTATOES**

2 medium russet potatoes, peeled and sliced into 1-inch chunks

2 cups vegetable oil

**ENCHILADAS**

12 homemade red chile corn tortillas (page 131)

14 ounces *queso fresco*, crumbled

½ white onion, finely chopped

4 cups chopped lettuce

2 Roma tomatoes, sliced into half moons

In a bowl, combine all the ingredients for the chipotle *crema*. Taste for salt. Cover and set aside. The *crema* is not traditionally served with these enchiladas, but it's tasty!

Transfer the potatoes to a bowl. Cover with water. Prep up all your fresh ingredients and cheese first. Cover and reserve.

In a large skillet, pour in the oil. Preheat to medium heat for 5 minutes. Drain and dry off the potatoes well. Fry them in the preheated oil for 20 minutes or until golden brown, crispy, and fork tender. Transfer them to a metal rack lined with a baking sheet. Place them in a low-temperature oven to keep them warm.

Pour out half of the oil from the skillet and return it to medium heat. Once it's hot, add 2 tortillas at a time. Cook for 15 to 20 seconds per side. You don't want the tortilla to get crispy at all, just soft and pliable. Place in between foil paper until all tortillas are cooked. Let tortillas steam for 2 minutes.

While tortillas are still warm, fill them each down the center with about 3 tablespoons of *queso fresco* and 2 teaspoons of minced onion. Roll as tight as you can and transfer to a serving plate. Spoon some *crema* onto each enchilada. Top with the remaining *queso fresco*. Serve with the fried potatoes on top. Add lettuce topped with tomatoes on the other side. Serve right away.

TIPS & VARIATIONS

- **These red chile corn tortilla enchiladas are not dipped or topped with any enchilada sauce. But I have to confess, I love a spicy Tomato Chile de Arbol Salsa (page 55) for garnish on my enchiladas with a side of Chiles Toreados & Cebollitas (page 124).**

TIPS & VARIATIONS

- **For a sweet-tart flavor, add cubed fresh pineapple in between the marinated pork before grilling.**
- **Country-style pork ribs are delicious marinated in *al pastor* adobo. Cover them and oven-roast at 350°F for 90 minutes. Uncover and roast for an additional 30 to 40 minutes. Baste once or twice with extra adobo as the ribs cook.**

# Brochetas al Pastor

**The next best thing to enjoying traditional pork *al pastor* is these charcoal-grilled kebabs. The smoky flavors of the pork with grilled pineapple, roasted tomatillo salsa, and grilled onions will keep you coming back for more tacos!**

PREP TIME: **40 MINUTES**
COOK TIME: **1 HOUR, 10 MINUTES**
YIELD: **6 SERVINGS**

2½ pounds pork butt or shoulder

Salt and pepper, to taste

1½ cups Al Pastor Adobo marinade (page 101)

1 fresh pineapple (3 pounds before peeling), sliced into rings

1 white onion, quartered

Vegetable oil, for brushing the grill

24 taqueria-size (4-inch) corn tortillas

1 cup minced cilantro

1 cup Roasted Tomatillo Salsa (page 54)

3 limes, sliced into wedges

Slice the pork into 2-inch pieces. Season lightly with salt and pepper and then mix in the marinade until everything is coated evenly. Cover and refrigerate for 6 hours.

Reserve 6 chunks of pineapple and 6 large pieces of onion for assembling the kebabs.

Skewer the meat on 6 heavy double-prong skewers. Add some of the reserved onion and pineapple to the bottom of the skewer. Set them aside.

Prepare your grill for direct and indirect cooking on high heat. When the grill is hot, brush the grates with vegetable oil. Grill the pineapple slices, turning as needed, for 10 minutes. Wrap the quartered onions in aluminum foil and place packets on the grill. Cook the onions for 25 minutes. Move the pineapple and onions over to the cool side once done.

Brush on a little more oil on the grates. Place the kebabs directly on the hot side of the grill. Cook for 20 minutes, turning as needed. The internal temperature should read 145°F. Then move the kebabs over to the cool side of the grill. Close the lid for 7 minutes.

Warm the corn tortillas directly on the grill for 1 to 2 minutes, turning as needed. Fill tacos with chopped *al pastor* pork, grilled pineapple and onions, cilantro, and the salsa. Finish with a squeeze of lime.

# Bistec en Salsa

Beefsteak in salsa or *bistec en salsa*? I have also seen it written as *bifstek*. They are slang terms that have evolved along the way that refer to beefsteak. Typically, the term refers to a cut of beef that is thin and that cooks quickly. There are endless recipes in Mexican cuisine where *bistec* is used to yield some of the most delicious dishes. Serve with refried beans and warm tortillas.

PREP TIME: **15 MINUTES**
COOK TIME: **30 MINUTES**
YIELD: **4 SERVINGS**

1 teaspoon salt

1 teaspoon pepper, plus more to taste

1 teaspoon granulated garlic

1½ pounds beef shoulder, chuck, skirt, or top round steaks

4 tablespoons avocado oil

½ medium white onion, thinly sliced

3 cloves garlic, minced

3 serrano peppers, thinly sliced

1½ cups Salsa Verde (page 96)

Handful of fresh cilantro

In a small bowl, mix the salt, pepper, and granulated garlic. Season the beef lightly on both sides.

In a skillet, heat 3 tablespoons of the oil over medium heat for a few minutes. When the oil is hot, brown the beef, turning as needed, for 7 to 8 minutes.

Move the beef to one side of the skillet. Add the onion, garlic, and serrano peppers. Season lightly with salt and pepper. Sauté for 3 minutes, then move the vegetables onto the beef.

Pour in the salsa, making sure the beef is covered. Add the fresh cilantro. Reduce the heat to a simmer. Cover and cook for 10 minutes.

TIPS & VARIATIONS

- **I suggest tenderizing the thin beefsteaks with a meat mallet before adding them to your recipes.**
- **Top round and bottom round steaks are lean and best suited for long cooking times.**
- **If you omit the salsa in this recipe and add more onion, it's *bistec encebollado*. Mix in serrano peppers, white onion, and tomato and you have *bistec á la Mexicana*. Coat the steaks in cracker meal or breadcrumbs and fry them. That is *milanesa*. Stew with lots of roasted green chile and potatoes and you have *bistec ranchero*. The possibilities are endless!**

# Tacos de Pescado

You know when you get a craving for a certain dish and you can't stop thinking about it? I had one of those cravings for fish tacos made with crispy fish — baked or broiled wasn't going to do it. It had to be Baja-style fish tacos. That's how this recipe came about, and I plan to make it again and again. Secret: the beer batter is key to the crispiness.

PREP TIME: **1 HOUR**
COOK TIME: **15 MINUTES**
YIELD: **4 SERVINGS**

**SLAW**

4 cups shredded cabbage

1 habanero pepper, minced

¼ cup minced cilantro

3 sliced green onions

2 tablespoons fresh lime juice (1 large lime)

3 tablespoons olive oil

Salt and pepper, to taste

***MORITA* MAYONNAISE**

½ cup mayonnaise

1 tablespoon fresh lime juice (½ large lime)

¼ cup Smoky Chile Morita Salsa (page 76)

Salt and white pepper, to taste

**FISH**

1 pound whitefish, catfish, mahi-mahi, or cod fillets

1 teaspoon lemon-pepper seasoning

1 cup all-purpose flour

½ teaspoon chipotle powder

½ teaspoon salt

½ teaspoon pepper

8 ounces lager-style beer

1½ teaspoons yellow mustard

2 cups canola oil, for frying

8 corn tortillas

**GARNISHES**

6 radishes, sliced thin

1 large avocado, sliced into thin wedges

3 limes, sliced into wedges

continues on page 140

continued from page 139

In a medium glass bowl, combine all the ingredients for the cabbage slaw. Stir well to combine, taste for salt, cover, and set aside.

In a small bowl, combine all the ingredients for the *morita* mayonnaise. Stir until smooth, taste for salt, cover, and set aside.

Cut the fish fillets in half, lengthwise, then cut in half crosswise so you have 4 pieces of each fillet. Pat the fish dry with paper towels. Transfer to a plate, season one side with lemon-pepper seasoning. Keep chilled until ready to use.

In a large bowl, add the flour and chipotle powder, salt, and pepper. Stir well. Gradually and gently whisk in the beer and mustard until most of the lumps are gone. Let the batter sit for 20 minutes in the refrigerator.

In a medium-size heavy pot, heat the oil to 375°F Add a few pieces of fish to the batter, making sure they are evenly coated. Shake off any excess batter from the fish and add one piece at a time to the hot oil. Fry 3 to 4 pieces at a time, making sure not to overcrowd the pan. Fry until golden brown, turning as needed, about 4 to 5 minutes. Use a spatula to remove the fillets and drain them on paper towels.

To plate, spread some sriracha mayo onto a warmed tortilla, top with 2 pieces of fish per taco, garnish with slaw, radishes, 1 to 2 slices of avocado, and lime wedges.

## TIPS & VARIATIONS

- **You can substitute sparkling mineral water for the beer.**
- **If you are having trouble getting the batter to stick to the fish, dredge the seasoned fish in all-purpose flour before dipping it into the batter.**
- **These tacos are delicious made with jumbo shrimp or bay scallops instead of fish.**

# Tostadas de Tinga

*Tinga* is a traditional dish from Puebla, Mexico. It is usually prepared with shredded chicken that has been cooked low and slow in a rich tomato sauce flavored with smoky chipotles in adobo. It is popular to serve *tinga* on tostadas, but it is delicious in tacos, *sopes*, burritos, enchiladas, and more!

PREP TIME: **25 MINUTES**
COOK TIME: **1 HOUR**
YIELD: **6 SERVINGS**

2 tablespoons avocado oil
1 medium white onion, thinly sliced
Salt and pepper, to taste
2 pounds cooked, shredded chicken breast
1 recipe for Mango Chipotle Salsa (page 28)
12 corn tortilla tostadas
4 cups shredded lettuce
1½ cups chopped Roma tomato
8 ounces *cotija* cheese, finely grated
8 ounces Mexican *crema*
2 large avocados, sliced
2 large limes, sliced into wedges

In a large skillet, heat the oil over medium heat for 2 minutes. Add the onion. Season lightly with salt and pepper. Sauté for 10 minutes, or until the onion begins to caramelize. Fold in the chicken, then pour in the chipotle salsa. Stir well to combine. Let the *tinga* cook until it reduces and thickens, 45 to 50 minutes.

Once the *tinga* has reduced, taste for seasoning. Layer the tostadas with the *tinga*, lettuce, tomato, cheese, *crema*, avocado, and a squeeze of lime juice. Serve right away.

TIPS & VARIATIONS

- **A quick way to prepare homemade tostadas is to bake them. Brush corn tortillas with oil on both sides. Place the tortillas on a baking sheet and bake in a 400°F oven for 15 to 20 minutes. Flip halfway through the cooking time. Once they are crispy, they are done.**
- **A simpler shredded beef *tinga* consists of finely chopped tomato and tomatillos combined with minced chipotle, lots of onion, and fresh garlic.**

# Tacos Dorados de Picadillo

This recipe for *picadillo con papas* (ground beef and potatoes) was a staple dish prepared by Mom quite often. It is versatile and can be used in a variety of ways. A tasty filling for tacos *dorados*, enchiladas, burritos, and especially Mom's awesome *chiles rellenos*!

PREP TIME: **35 MINUTES**
COOK TIME: **50 MINUTES**
YIELD: **6 SERVINGS**

3 tablespoons avocado oil

1 medium russet potato, skin on, finely chopped

1 pound ground chuck or sirloin, 80% lean

¾ teaspoon salt

¾ teaspoon pepper

¾ teaspoon garlic powder

¾ teaspoon cumin

½ teaspoon oregano

3 cloves garlic, minced

1 cup chopped white onion

2 large Roma tomatoes, coarsely chopped

1 serrano pepper, coarsely chopped

12 corn tortillas

1¼ cups vegetable oil, for frying

**GARNISHES**

4 cups shredded lettuce

10 ounces *queso fresco*, crumbled, or 6 ounces Chihuahua cheese, shredded

1 cup Spicy Jalapeño Salsa (page 45)

2 cups Pico de Gallo salsa (page 25)

In a nonstick pan, preheat the avocado oil to medium heat. Add the potatoes and cook until golden brown. Transfer the potatoes to a plate lined with paper towels. Reserve.

In a separate skillet, at medium to high heat, add the ground beef. Season with the salt, pepper, garlic powder, cumin, and oregano. Crumble and cook for 8 minutes. Add the garlic and onion. Saute for 4 minutes.

Add the tomatoes, peppers, and ¼ cup of water to a blender, and blend on high until smooth. Pour into the skillet with the beef. Fold in the potatoes. Stir well to combine. Cook at a steady simmer for 10 minutes. Remove from the heat and cool.

Warm the corn tortillas on a preheated griddle set to medium-high heat until soft. In a separate skillet, preheat the vegetable oil at medium heat. Wrap the warm tortillas in a towel. Fill each tortilla with 3 tablespoons of *picadillo*. Fold over like a taco and transfer to a plate.

Fry the tacos in the preheated oil until crispy, turning as needed. Transfer the fried tacos, standing up, to a bowl lined with paper towels. Open the tacos and garnish with the shredded lettuce, *queso fresco* or Chihuahua cheese, Spicy Jalapeño Salsa, and fresh Pico de Gallo salsa.

# Mulitas de Carne Asada

*Mulitas* is Spanish for "little mules." I imagine they call these *mulitas* because they are packed on either side of the tortillas.

Corn tortillas prepared from freshly ground corn *masa* are the best! But I have to say that I am very happy with the *masa harina* version, certainly compared with a store-bought tortilla. One *mulita* is pretty filling. They are best served hot off the griddle.

**PREP TIME: 15 MINUTES**
**COOK TIME: 20 MINUTES**
**YIELD: 2 SERVINGS**

1 pound chuck, skirt, or flap steak
¾ teaspoon coarse sea salt
¾ teaspoon freshly ground black pepper
3 teaspoons avocado oil
8 corn tortillas
6 ounces Oaxaca or Chihuahua cheese, shredded
Guacamole y Totopos (page 133)
½ cup Creamy Taqueria-Style Salsa (page 53)
½ cup finely chopped white onion
⅓ cup minced cilantro
2 limes, sliced into wedges

Preheat a 12-inch cast-iron skillet to medium heat for 4 to 5 minutes or until you see a wisp of smoke. Season the steak on both sides lightly with the salt and pepper. Drizzle with the oil all over. When the pan begins to smoke lightly, sear the steak for 3 to 4 minutes per side for medium-rare. For medium steak, cook 2 minutes longer. Transfer the steak to a cutting board and let it rest for 5 minutes. Slice thin and against the grain.

Place 4 tortillas on a preheated griddle set to medium heat. Add 2 tablespoons of shredded cheese to each tortilla. Add 4 ounces of sliced steak to each tortilla. Add 1½ tablespoons of guacamole on top of the steak. Top with 2 more tablespoons of cheese. Place another tortilla on top. Heat just until the cheese begins to melt on the bottom. Flip over and cook for another 30 to 45 seconds.

I enjoy separating each *mulita* and garnishing both sides with the salsa, onion, and a squeeze of lime.

### TIPS & VARIATIONS

- **If assembling larger servings of *mulitas*, it's much faster on an outdoor flat-top grill. If you have a good-quality corn tortilla, you can prepare ahead by warming the stacked tortillas with just cheese and steak. Store them in an airtight container in the refrigerator until you are ready to reheat. Reheat *mulitas* on a preheated griddle set to medium until the cheese melts and ingredients are warmed through. Add guacamole and garnishes afterward.**
- ***Mulitas* can be filled with any of your favorite cuts of beef, seafood, chicken, pork, and vegetarian options, including Chiles Toreados & Cebollitas (page 124).**

# Tacos Gobernador

Tacos *gobernador* literally translates to "governor's tacos"! What? Well, if these shrimp tacos are good enough for the governor of Sinaloa, Mexico, then they are certainly good enough to share! What's not to love about a cheesy shrimp taco on homemade corn tortillas? It's a must-try for your next taco night!

**PREP TIME: 25 MINUTES**
**COOK TIME: 40 MINUTES**
**YIELD: 6 SERVINGS**

- 3 tablespoons unsalted butter
- ½ cup chopped onion
- 4 cloves garlic, minced
- 1 large serrano pepper, minced
- Salt and pepper, to taste
- 3 Roma tomatoes, chopped
- 1 large roasted poblano pepper, chopped
- 2 pounds uncooked shrimp, cleaned and deveined
- 2 tablespoons fresh lime juice (1 large lime)
- 12 ounces Chihuahua, Oaxaca, or Jack cheese, shredded
- 12 corn tortillas
- 1 cup Toasted Chile de Arbol Tomatillo Salsa (page 56)

Add the butter to a skillet over medium heat. Add the onion, garlic, and serrano pepper. Season lightly with salt and pepper. Sauté for 3 minutes.

Add the tomato and poblano pepper to the skillet. Sauté for another 4 minutes.

Mix in the shrimp and lime juice. Season lightly with salt and pepper. Cook for 3 minutes. Remove from the heat and reserve in the skillet, covered.

On a preheated nonstick griddle at medium heat, add 4 ounces of the shredded cheese into two separate mounds, directly to the nonstick surface. Once cheese begins to melt, lay a corn tortilla on top of each cheese mound. After 35 seconds, carefully flip the tortillas over. To each tortilla, spoon in 4 shrimp with some of the sauce.

Using a spatula, fold over like a taco and continue cooking. The oils from the cheese will coat the tortillas a little. Continue cooking until desired crispiness of tacos. Repeat with the remaining tortillas and serve right away with the salsa.

## TIPS & VARIATIONS

- **Easy roasted poblano peppers: Rub a light coat of oil all over a fresh poblano pepper. On a baking sheet, transfer under the broiler set on high heat. Broil for 8 to 10 minutes, turning over halfway through the cooking time. Wrap the pepper in a kitchen towel for 10 minutes. Remove blistered skin, seeds, and stem.**
- **Not crazy about seafood? Substitute the shrimp with shredded chicken *tinga* (page 141) or Slow Cooker Pork Carnitas (page 40).**

TIPS & VARIATIONS

- **The steaming method is the way my parents cooked beef cheek, but other cooking methods work well too. You can cook the meat in a slow cooker for 8 hours. If you want to use a pressure cooker, put the seasoned beef cheek in the pressure cooker, add 7 cups of water, sliced onion, and fresh garlic. Cook for 1 hour and 45 minutes at medium heat.**
- **My favorite way to enjoy leftover *barbacoa* like this is to cook it in a spicy *salsa roja* or *salsa verde*. This makes a delicious filling for tacos, burritos, *sopes*, tostadas, and even tamales!**

# Barbacoa de Cachete

*Barbacoa de cachete* is beef cheek that has been perfectly steamed. In my opinion, these are some of the best beef tacos you will experience. The taste takes me back to my family roots, especially to the foods cooked for special days, for Sunday brunch after church, or for trip to *la pulga* (flea market). I know there are lots of variations of *barbacoa* recipes online; this one is simple, with not much prep involved.

PREP TIME: **20 MINUTES**
COOK TIME: **4 HOURS**
YIELD: **6 SERVINGS**

4 pounds beef cheek

2 teaspoons salt

2 teaspoons freshly ground black pepper

18 corn tortillas

1 large white onion, finely chopped

2 ounces cilantro, minced

3 limes, sliced into wedges

1 cup Mom's Toasted Chile de Arbol Salsa (page 72)

1 cup Tomato Chile de Arbol Salsa (page 55)

1 cup Salsa Cruda (page 32)

Trim away some of the excess fat from the beef cheek. Slice and divide into 2 equal portions. Season each portion with 1 teaspoon of the salt and 1 teaspoon of the pepper. Wrap each portion tightly in a double layer of foil paper.

Fill the bottom of the steamer pot with water to the indicated line. Place the steamer insert in place. Heat the steamer pot on high. Place the beef cheek packets into the steamer pot and cover. When it comes to a rapid steam/boil, reduce to medium heat. Continue cooking for 4 hours. The beef cheek should pull apart easily with a fork when ready. Take one packet out and check for tenderness. If it is still tough, steam for 30 more minutes.

When ready, remove the beef cheek packets from the steamer and carefully transfer to a large sheet pan to cool for 10 minutes. Carefully open the packets and drain the fat and broth rendered during cooking into another bowl. Transfer the beef to a serving bowl. Pour in ¾ cup of reserved broth with fat into the meat. Stir gently to combine. Discard the remaining broth. Warm the corn tortillas on a preheated griddle set to medium for 1 minute per side, or until warm and soft. Transfer the tortillas to a tortilla warmer or wrap them in a clean kitchen towel. To each tortilla, add 4 ounces of beef cheek. Garnish with the chopped onion, minced cilantro, a squeeze of lime, and the salsas.

# Cochinita Pibil Panuchos

Bring the flavors of Yucatan into your kitchen with this delicious recipe for *panuchos*. *Panuchos* are freshly prepared corn tortillas stuffed with black beans and fried until crispy. They are topped with sour-orange-and-*achiote*-marinated shredded pork, pickled red onions, and roasted habanero salsa.

PREP TIME: **45 MINUTES**
COOK TIME: **1 HOUR, 35 MINUTES**
YIELD: **6 SERVINGS**

2 pounds pork butt

Salt and pepper, to taste

12 freshly prepared corn tortillas (page 131)

1½ cups refried beans, preferably black

1 cup plus 3 tablespoons vegetable oil, for frying

2 sections prepared banana leaves, 11-by-14-inch each (see Tips & Variations, page 149)

1 cup Cochinita Pibil Adobo (page 108)

2 cups shredded lettuce

2 Roma tomatoes, thinly sliced

1 large avocado, sliced into thin wedges

Pickled Red Onions (page 127)

½ cup Salsa de Habanero con Vinagre (page 61)

Slice the pork into 3-inch pieces. Season lightly with salt and pepper, then let sit at room temperature for 45 minutes.

In the meantime, mix the *masa* (dough) for the corn tortillas and roll the dough into 10 equal-size balls. Cover with a damp dish towel or plastic wrap. Preheat a large griddle to medium-high heat.

When the griddle is hot, flatten the *masa* balls, one at a time, using a tortilla press lined with plastic. Cook each tortilla for 15 seconds, flip, then cook for 30 to 35 seconds, and flip for a third time. The tortilla should inflate at this point. Repeat with the remaining *masa* balls until all are cooked.

Transfer the tortillas to a plate and carefully slice each one open to create a pocket. Using a butter knife, spread 2 tablespoons of the refried beans inside each one. Press shut. Cover and set aside.

After 45 minutes, add 3 tablespoons of the oil to a pressure cooker and heat to medium for 3 to 5 minutes. Sear and brown the pork pieces in batches, then transfer them to a plate.

Once all the pork is browned, add 4 cups of water to the cooker. Place one section of softened banana leaves at the bottom. Add the pork. Pour in the adobo. Cover with the remaining banana leaves.

Secure and lock the lid. Turn the heat to high. Once the pressure cooker locks and begins to cook under high pressure, reduce the heat to medium-low.

After 45 minutes, remove the pressure cooker from the heat. Let stand until the safety valve releases. Open the cooker and transfer the pork to a serving dish. Shred the pork and ladle in some of the broth from the pressure cooker. Cover to keep warm.

In a large skillet over medium heat, preheat the remaining 1 cup of oil for 3 minutes. Fry the *panuchos* until crispy. Transfer them to a plate lined with paper towels.

To serve, layer with lettuce, pork, sliced tomato, 1 to 2 slices of avocado, pickled red onions, and the salsa.

## TIPS & VARIATIONS

- **To soften the fresh banana leaves, place them in a preheated 250°F oven for 20 minutes. They will turn from opaque green to a shiny green color when ready.**
- **To prepare this recipe in a slow cooker, add water, banana leaves, and seared pork to the slow cooker. Cover with the remaining banana leaves. Cook on low for 8 hours.**

# Acknowledgments

My dad's dream of owning and running a successful family food business was always present in my mind during this whole journey. In a way, I feel that Mom, Dad, and my siblings all play a part in what I share in this book.

Dad instilled in us the belief that hard work pays off and that you should never give up on your dreams. He was born in Mexico, but his birthday happened to be on the Fourth of July. He was a proud Mexican man living in America, where he experienced many opportunities throughout his life.

Mom was the devoted housewife, mother, and, in my eyes, the best Mexican cook. We grew up poor, but rich in so many ways. She will never know how that simple bowl of *fideo* with pinto beans and warm tortillas would shape me into the person I have become today. I cannot thank them enough for being the best mom and dad.

I started this Mexican food journey more than seventeen years ago with the intention of keeping their memory alive. Their legacy continues in every single recipe I share. Thank you, Mom and Dad.

Thank you to the tight-knit community of Hispanic food bloggers that I have had the pleasure of knowing and learning from throughout the years. Even though we may all share a similar passion for the dishes that we grew up with, we all a have our own unique story to tell.

A huge thank-you to the brands that saw something in me and trusted me to deliver their love and passion for their products. And finally, thank you for the encouraging words, support, and endless taste-testing and experimentation sessions: Kity, Vicky, Janet, Ismael, Crystal, my *primos* in Mexico, Patty, Santiago, Nicolas, Richard, and my loyal followers! I am blown away by your love and kindness!

# Glossary

***Abuela*** grandmother

***Achiote*** red paste made from annatto seeds

***Ahogados*** drowned in salsa

***Al pastor*** shepard style

***Ancho*** is a poblano pepper dried

***Barbacoa*** beef or lamb slow cooked

***Baracoa de cachete*** beef cheek slow cooked

***Birria*** a flavorful meat stew

***Birria de res*** a flavorful meat stew made with beef

***Bistec*** beefsteak

***Bistec en salsa*** beefsteak in salsa

***Bolillos*** bread rolls

***Brochetas*** kebabs, skewers

***Caldillo*** a light sauce

***Caldillo de jitomate*** a light sauce prepared with Roma tomatoes

***Camarón*** shrimp

***Camarónes*** shrimp, plural

***Canela*** cinnamon

***Carnitas*** fried pork shoulder chunks

***Carne asada*** grilled meats

***Cascabel*** a round or bell-shape dried chile pepper

***Cebollitas*** fresh knob onions

***Chamoy*** a liquid or paste made from fruits and dried chile peppers, a condiment

***Chicharrones*** fried pork skins

***Chilaca*** a long and skinny green chile pepper

***Chilaquiles*** fried corn tortillas in salsa

***Chile colorado*** description of the red dried chile peppers, typically *ancho*, *guajillo*

***Chile de arbol*** bird peppers, peppers from a tree

***Chile limon*** a lime and spicy red dried chile pepper seasoning

***Chile meco*** a type of chipotle pepper

***Chile morita*** a type of chipotle pepper

***Chile piquin*** small round chile pepper, both fresh and dried

***Chile seco*** dried chile peppers

***Chiles rellenos*** stuffed chile peppers

***Chiles toreados*** blistered peppers

***Chiltepin*** intensely hot small round chile pepper popular in northern Mexico

***Chorizo Norteño*** Northern Mexico–style pork sausage

***Cochinita pibil*** slow-roasted marinated pork popular in the Yucatan

***Comarónes á la diabla*** deviled shrimp

***Comino*** cumin

***Cotija*** a hard crumbly salty cheese

***Crema*** Mexican-style sour cream

***Curtido*** thinly sliced pickled onions or cabbage

***Encebollado*** a dish prepared with a lot of onion

***Entomatadas*** fried corn tortillas dipped in a tomato sauce, then filled and rolled

***Epazote*** an aromatic herb used in soups and stews

**Escabeche** pickling of vegetables and some savory dishes

**Fideo** a vermicelli-style pasta

**Frijoles charros** ranch-style beans with bacon and sometimes beer

**Gobernador** governor

**Guajillo** a mild dried red chile used mostly for its red color

**Güero** a yellow waxy chile pepper

**Guisada** sautéed or stewed

**Guisados** stews

**Hojas de laurel** bay leaves

**Huevos rancheros** fried eggs on crispy corn tortillas

**Jengibre** ginger

**La cena** dinner

**La comida** lunch

**Masa** a dough prepared with ground field corn or dough prepared with wheat flour

**Masa harina** instant corn flour for tortillas

**Mejorana** marjoram

**Molcajete** a mortar and pestle carved from volcanic stone

**Mulato** a large dried pepper that looks almost black in color

**Mulitas** a stacked taco with corn tortillas

**Negro** black

**Nogada** a creamy white sauce prepared with walnuts

**Nopalitos** cactus paddles, sliced

**Panuchos** a black bean–stuffed corn tortilla lightly fried and topped with pork

**Pasilla** a dried chile pepper, long and skinny, almost black in color

**Pepitas** pumpkin seeds without the shell

**Picadillo** stewed ground beef

**Pico de gallo** rooster's beak, a green, white, and red chunky fresh salsa

**Pimieta dulce** allspice

**Pimieta negra** peppercorns

**Pipián** a red or green sauce prepared with toasted pumpkin seeds

**Primo** cousin

**Puerco** pork

**Queso** cheese

**Queso en salsa** cheese in salsa

**Queso fesco** fresh cheese

**Queso panela** farmer's cheese

**Rajas** strips

**Recad** a sauce for marinating

**Romero** rosemary

**Salsa cruda** raw salsa

**Salsa de mesa** table salsa

**Salsa fresca** fresh salsa

**Salsa roja** red salsa

**Salsa verde** green salsa

**Semilla** seed

**Sopes** corn dough round cakes

**Taquitos** rolled fried tacos

**Taquiza** taco party

**Tejolote** stone pestle

**Tia** aunt

**Tinga** a dish prepared with shredded meat in a chipotle sauce

**Tomillo** thyme

**Totopos** corn tortilla chips

# Index

# About the Author

My name is Sonia Mendez Garcia. I grew up in a large, loving Mexican family, where the kitchen was always a focal point. I learned basic salsa recipes as a teenager, and it became my passion. My goal is to inspire you to explore and discover some of the most most authentic and traditional flavors from my kitchen to yours. Find many more recipes in my food blog, La Piña en La Cocina.

weldon**owen**
an imprint of Insight Editions
P.O. Box 3088
San Rafael, CA 94912
www.weldonowen.com

**CEO** Raoul Goff
**SVP Group Publisher** Jeff McLaughlin
**VP Publisher** Roger Shaw
**Executive Editor** Edward Ash-Milby
**Assistant Editor** Kayla Belser
**Managing Editor** Michelle Hope
**VP Creative** Chrissy Kwasnik
**Art Director** Megan Sinead Bingham
**Production Design** Jean Hwang
**VP Manufacturing** Alix Nicholaeff
**Senior Production Manager** Joshua Smith
**Strategic Production Planner** Lina s Palma-Temena

**Interior Design** Malea Clark-Nicholson

**Photographer** Lorena Masso
**Food Stylist** Victoria Woollard
**Food Stylist Assistant** Penny Eng

Weldon Owen would also like to thank Margaret Parrish and Dominik Sklarzyk.

Text © 2025 Sonia Mendez Garcia

All rights reserved. No part of this book may be reproduced in any form without written permission from the publisher.

ISBN: 979-8-88674-323-4

Manufactured in China by Insight Editions
10 9 8 7 6 5 4 3 2 1

Insight Editions, in association with Roots of Peace, will plant two trees for each tree used in the manufacturing of this book. Roots of Peace is an internationally renowned humanitarian organization dedicated to eradicating land mines worldwide and converting war-torn lands into productive farms and wildlife habitats. Roots of Peace will plant two million fruit and nut trees in Afghanistan and provide farmers there with the skills and support necessary for sustainable land use.